ONE FLIGHT AWAY: AN EXAMINATION OF THE THREAT POSED BY ISIS TERRORISTS WITH WESTERN PASSPORTS

HEARING

BEFORE THE

SUBCOMMITTEE ON BORDER AND MARITIME SECURITY

OF THE

COMMITTEE ON HOMELAND SECURITY HOUSE OF REPRESENTATIVES

ONE HUNDRED THIRTEENTH CONGRESS

SECOND SESSION

SEPTEMBER 10, 2014

Serial No. 113–84

Printed for the use of the Committee on Homeland Security

Available via the World Wide Web: http://www.gpo.gov/fdsys/

U.S. GOVERNMENT PUBLISHING OFFICE

92–901 PDF   WASHINGTON : 2015

For sale by the Superintendent of Documents, U.S. Government Publishing Office
Internet: bookstore.gpo.gov Phone: toll free (866) 512–1800; DC area (202) 512–1800
Fax: (202) 512–2104 Mail: Stop IDCC, Washington, DC 20402–0001

COMMITTEE ON HOMELAND SECURITY

MICHAEL T. McCAUL, Texas, *Chairman*

LAMAR SMITH, Texas
PETER T. KING, New York
MIKE ROGERS, Alabama
PAUL C. BROUN, Georgia
CANDICE S. MILLER, Michigan, *Vice Chair*
PATRICK MEEHAN, Pennsylvania
JEFF DUNCAN, South Carolina
TOM MARINO, Pennsylvania
JASON CHAFFETZ, Utah
STEVEN M. PALAZZO, Mississippi
LOU BARLETTA, Pennsylvania
RICHARD HUDSON, North Carolina
STEVE DAINES, Montana
SUSAN W. BROOKS, Indiana
SCOTT PERRY, Pennsylvania
MARK SANFORD, South Carolina
CURTIS CLAWSON, Florida

BENNIE G. THOMPSON, Mississippi
LORETTA SANCHEZ, California
SHEILA JACKSON LEE, Texas
YVETTE D. CLARKE, New York
BRIAN HIGGINS, New York
CEDRIC L. RICHMOND, Louisiana
WILLIAM R. KEATING, Massachusetts
RON BARBER, Arizona
DONDALD M. PAYNE, JR., New Jersey
BETO O'ROURKE, Texas
FILEMON VELA, Texas
ERIC SWALWELL, California
VACANCY
VACANCY

BRENDAN P. SHIELDS, *Staff Director*
JOAN O'HARA, *Acting Chief Counsel*
MICHAEL S. TWINCHEK, *Chief Clerk*
I. LANIER AVANT, *Minority Staff Director*

———

SUBCOMMITTEE ON BORDER AND MARITIME SECURITY

CANDICE S. MILLER, Michigan, *Chairwoman*

JEFF DUNCAN, South Carolina
TOM MARINO, Pennsylvania
STEVEN M. PALAZZO, Mississippi
LOU BARLETTA, Pennsylvania
CURTIS CLAWSON, Florida
MICHAEL T. McCAUL, Texas *(Ex Officio)*

SHEILA JACKSON LEE, Texas
LORETTA SANCHEZ, California
BETO O'ROURKE, Texas
VACANCY
BENNIE G. THOMPSON, Mississippi *(Ex Officio)*

PAUL L. ANSTINE, II, *Subcommittee Staff Director*
DEBORAH JORDAN, *Subcommittee Clerk*
ALISON NORTHROP, *Minority Subcommittee Staff Director*

CONTENTS

ONE FLIGHT AWAY: AN EXAMINATION OF THE THREAT POSED BY ISIS TERRORISTS WITH WESTERN PASSPORTS

Wednesday, September 10, 2014

U.S. HOUSE OF REPRESENTATIVES,
SUBCOMMITTEE ON BORDER AND MARITIME SECURITY,
COMMITTEE ON HOMELAND SECURITY,
Washington, DC.

The subcommittee met, pursuant to call, at 10:04 a.m., in Room 311, Cannon House Office Building, Hon. Candice S. Miller [Chairwoman of the subcommittee] presiding.

Present: Representatives Miller, Duncan, Barletta, Clawson, Thompson, Jackson Lee, and O'Rourke.

Mrs. MILLER. The Committee on Homeland Security, the Subcommittee on Border and Maritime Security will come to order.

The subcommittee is meeting today to examine the threat posed by ISIS foreign fighters who are holding Western passports. We are very pleased today to be joined by Mr. Troy Miller, who is the acting assistant commissioner at the U.S. Customs and Border Protection. Mr. John Wagner, a frequent testifier to our subcommittee here, and we appreciate him coming back. He is the assistant commissioner at the U.S. Customs and Border Protection.

Ms. Jennifer Lasley—we welcome you, the deputy under secretary for analysis at DHS's Office of Intelligence and Analysis. Ms. Hillary Johnson, the acting deputy coordinator for homeland security and multilateral affairs at the State Department's Bureau of Counterterrorism. I will introduce them a bit more formally shortly.

Tomorrow marks the 13th anniversary of the most heinous and cowardly attack in the history of our Nation, certainly a terrorist attack that took the lives of nearly 3,000 of our fellow Americans. It happened in part because our visa security and border security defenses were not very effective. Among the most important weaknesses that the attackers were able to exploit was our porous outer ring of border security. In total, the 19 hijackers passed through the U.S. border security 68 times back and forth without being detected.

On that day in September, we learned a very hard lesson. As noted by the 9/11 commission, "For terrorists, travel documents are as important as weapons." I think that is a very, very important statement by them. It is so true.

Many more terrorists since have exploited the visa system in one fashion or another, and it is an on-going vulnerability, certainly

(1)

one heightened by the significant growing threat that the Islamic State of Iraq and Syria pose to our Nation. Our best estimates are that thousands of individuals carrying Western passports have joined in the fight in Syria and in Iraq, including several hundred Americans.

Two innocent American journalists, James Foley and Steven Sotloff, were brutally beheaded by an ISIS terrorist who is likely a British citizen. These thugs have no regard for life and have threatened to attack our homeland, and the United States Government must be prepared to prevent such an act from happening. Terrorists with Western passports pose an additional risk to the homeland because many are eligible for visa-free travel through the Visa Waiver Program. Terrorists could be just one visa-free flight away from arriving in the United States, bringing with them their skills and their training and their ideology and their commitment to killing Americans, all these things that they have learned overseas.

Let us remember that Zacharias Moussaoui, the so-called 20th hijacker, actually traveled on the Visa Waiver Program before he enrolled in a Minneapolis flight school. Richard Reed, the shoe bomber who tried to ignite explosives in his shoe, also traveled on the Visa Waiver Program. Ramzi Yousef, who was one of the main perpetrators of the 1993 World Trade Center bombing, again used the Visa Waiver Program to enter the country.

These attacks occurred before the advent of increased scrutiny on the visa waiver countries. While I think we are confident that we can identify many threats today through the electronic system for travel authorization, commonly called ESTA—we will be talking about ESTA quite a bit in our hearing today—which all these waiver applicants have to fill out, it is clear that we may have trouble determining if some individuals have traveled to terrorist regions.

Although CBP continuously vets all visa applicants against our terrorism holdings, that information is imperfect if we do not have a complete picture of an individual's travel route. Collecting more information up front could be very, very helpful for us to do just that.

Patriot and other pilot programs that look at the totality of data on an ESTA and visa application are certainly good tools to help close some of our intelligence gaps and make connections that we would otherwise miss. However, critical information sharing, especially with our European allies, is critical to help combat the threat of foreign fighters bound for the United States. Unfortunately, Europe as a whole has been reluctant to share certain passenger name record data, or PNR data, as we call it, with the United States, and such a gap certainly puts our citizens in the United States at risk.

I want to commend our allies in the United Kingdom, who have been quick to realize the severity of the threat, especially as many Brits are among the ISIS fighters. We must work with our foreign allies like the United Kingdom and others to quickly identify those radicalized by ISIS and similar groups and prevent them from traveling to the United States.

Like the United Kingdom, I also think we should be looking at the authority that we have or we may need—and that will be a big part of our discussion here this morning—to revoke passports of American citizens who go to fight in ISIS. We need to reduce their ability to travel to the United States, and I think we need to consider what it will take to strip passports from those who provide support to or fight with terrorists.

I certainly look forward to hearing from our witnesses today on what further changes we have made in our visa security system to combat the threat of foreign fighters who travel often overland through neighboring Turkey's porous border, into Syria and into Iraq before returning home to Europe. It might be hard for many Americans to comprehend, but for many in Europe, traveling to Syria is as simple as just getting in their car and driving there.

Today's hearing is really about one simple question. Can the United States Government adequately detect terrorists' travel patterns, identify suspicious movement, and prevent those who would do us harm from coming into the United States? How can we best protect our homeland? Our enemies are intent on attacking our country and are actively seeking to avoid our countermeasures. We need to be one step ahead instead of constantly reacting to their latest attack.

Defeating terrorists' ability to move internationally has long been a focus area for this subcommittee. Terrorists who have plotted horrific attacks against us have crossed the U.S. border for training or fraudulently obtaining a student or a work visa. There are certainly further opportunities that we can take to prevent attacks and to limit terrorists' mobility, and that is why we are holding this hearing today. Our visa security process obviously needs to be robust, and we must deny terrorists freedom of movement because 13 years ago, we unfortunately saw what failure looked like.

The Chairwoman would now recognize the Ranking Minority Member of this subcommittee, the gentlelady from Texas, Ms. Jackson Lee, for her opening statement.

Ms. JACKSON LEE. Good morning. Let me thank the Chairwoman for yielding. Let me also acknowledge the Ranking Member of the full committee, Mr. Thompson, and thank him for his leadership, as he is joined by the Chairman of the full committee, Mr. McCaul, and the way that they have worked diligently to provide leadership in securing the homeland.

As I often remind our colleagues and as often as we are questioned by our constituents, the Homeland Security Committee is a pivotal committee that stands in the gap, making sure that the needs of our Nation, domestic needs in protecting the homeland, are the priority and recognized by the American people as having a department and a committee that is clearly assigned to protect the homeland.

September 11 continues to be a symbol for all of the untoward terrorists across and around the world. They view that as a challenge to them every year, as to whether or not they can continue to intimidate the Western world, and of course, the United States of America. Our values are contrary to their beliefs, and therefore, 9/11 poses for all of us a time of recognition that we still remain in the eye of the storm, and we must be diligent.

I would offer to say that we will not fall victim to the terrorists' intent, and that is that we will not terrorize ourselves. We will be vigilant, which I believe is extremely important, but we will be fair and just, and we will recognize the civil liberties of all.

But we are in some very challenging and difficult times, and so I want to thank the Chairwoman for allowing us and this committee in working with me and the full committee to be the very first committee that is addressing the question of ISIS here in the United States Congress upon our return. That is an important statement, for Homeland Security, Armed Services, the Intelligence Committee are the cornerstone of defending this Nation, and our collaboration and working together is key. That we are doing.

This fact-finding hearing will lay the groundwork for many other hearings that will be necessary to expeditiously address this question. This evening, the President will address the Nation and discuss new protocols as to how we confront ISIS, and as he has indicated, degrade and end ISIS. So I am not willing to cede the point that ISIS does not represent a threat to the United States.

I did not say imminent. I did not say today. But I believe this hearing recognizes that ISIS is a threat to the United States and to the people of the United States. Again, not in the instance of being intimidated, but being prepared to protect the people of the United States of America.

Like all Americans, I was horrified, outraged, and saddened by the beheadings of two American journalists, James Foley and Steven Sotloff, by ISIL terrorists in Syria. ISIL has used ruthless, brutal remedies and tactics to expand its control over areas of northwestern Iraq, northeastern Syria, threatening the security of both countries. They have attacked, killed, kidnapped, and displaced thousands of religious and ethnic minorities in the region, including Christians and including small ethnic minority groups.

U.S. officials have warned that Syria-based terrorist extremists may also pose a direct threat to our homeland. One concern is that foreign fighters holding Western passports might travel to this country to carry out a terrorist attack. Additionally, our own U.S. citizens are known to have likewise left the United States and gone to the battlefield to perpetrate jihad.

The total number of armed opposition fighters engaged with various groups in Syria, including ISIL, is estimated at between 75,000 to 100,000 persons. Of those, the U.S. Government estimates 12,000 are foreign fighters. Among those foreign fighters are estimated to be more than 1,000 individuals from Europe and over 100 from the United States, with about a dozen American fighters with ISIL specifically.

We may be reminded on 9/11, the count was approximately 19 who created the most heinous terrorist act, killing over 3,000 here in the United States of America. We mourn for them and their families.

Many have expressed particular concern about Western foreign fighters because they hold passports from countries that participate in the Visa Waiver Program, which generally allows them to travel to the United States without accepting—without obtaining a visa. I want assurances today that these individuals have been appropriately watch-listed, and I want to discuss and look at whether or not we need to make the No-Fly List more robust and would look to the idea of legislation quickly passed that makes sure that we shore up the No-Fly List, not to undermine civil liberties but to protect the Nation. I am interested in a discussion of that going forward in Classified or what is available today.

I would note, however, that while these waiver travelers usually do not need a visa to visit this country, they are currently vetted both prior to departure and upon arrival to the United States. I expect that we will discuss that process in more detail at this hearing. Similarly, some are concerned about U.S. citizens who travel to the fight and then seek to return to the country by air. We are aware of two individual suicide bombers from the United States who recently died in battle.

I expect discussion today about what DHS and its Federal partners can do to address such situations beyond adding individuals to the No-Fly List, if and when the need arises. Indeed, the Departments of Homeland Security and State play a vital role in disrupting terrorists' travel to the United States.

This subcommittee has previously examined U.S. visa security and passenger prescreening programs which are essential to addressing the foreign fighter threat to the homeland. I hope our DHS and State Department witnesses can speak to us about how these programs operate and how they can be used to address concerns regarding the VWP travel specifically.

I also hope to hear from our State Department witnesses about how we engage—and how we are engaging with our foreign partners to help address information gaps regarding individuals of concern and their travel patterns. Like Chairwoman Miller, I am glad that Europe is standing up. I believe that they should stand up and collaborate. While we maintain our values, we can secure this Nation.

While the United States cannot resolve the larger situation in Syria and Iraq in its totality, we can do it collaboratively with our Mideast allies and our Western allies. We do have the responsibility to protect the homeland from threats from ISIL and similar terrorist organizations. Be mindful—as we mourn and commemorate 9/11, be mindful of the fact that we have work to do.

I therefore strongly encourage the administration and Congressional leadership to ensure that all relevant committees, including Intelligence, Armed Services, and Homeland Security, are included in briefings so that there can be a collaborative strategy in conjunction with the administration, so we can work collaboratively together and address these issues. I know that our Chairpersons and Ranking Members are prepared to do so.

Finally, I look forward to the President's address to the Nation tonight as he outlines his plan for combatting ISIL. I remain committed to working with any of my colleagues on this committee and will look forward to the appropriate legislation that we would hope will be expedited and passed to ensure the safety and security of the homeland. It is our duty and it is our challenge.

With that, I yield back the balance of my time.

[The statement of Ranking Member Jackson Lee follows:]

STATEMENT OF RANKING MEMBER SHEILA JACKSON LEE

SEPTEMBER 10, 2014

I am pleased to join Chairwoman Miller in holding today's hearing to discuss the Federal Government's efforts to identify foreign fighters in Syria and Iraq who may seek to travel to the United States to do our Nation harm. This hearing could not be more timely.

Like all Americans, I was horrified, outraged, and saddened by the beheadings of two American journalists—James Foley and Steven Sotloff—by ISIL terrorists in Syria. ISIL has used ruthless, brutal tactics to expand its control over areas of northwestern Iraq and northeastern Syria, threatening the security of both countries.

They have attacked, killed, kidnapped, and displaced thousands of religious and ethnic minorities in the region, including Christians and Yazidis. U.S. officials have warned that Syria-based terrorist extremists may also pose a direct threat to our homeland.

One concern is that foreign fighters holding Western passports might travel to this country to carry out a terrorist attack. The total number of armed opposition fighters engaged with various groups in Syria, including ISIL, is estimated at between 75,000 and 110,000 persons. Of those, the U.S. Government estimates 12,000 are foreign fighters.

Among these foreign fighters are estimated to be more than 1,000 individuals from Europe and over 100 from the United States, with about a dozen Americans fighting with ISIL specifically. Many have expressed particular concern about Western foreign fighters, because they hold passports from countries that participate in the Visa Waiver Program (VWP), which generally allows them to travel to the United States without obtaining a visa.

I want assurances today that these individuals have been appropriately watchlisted and placed on the No-Fly List, and would welcome the opportunity to discuss their status in more detail outside of this open setting if necessary. I would note, however, that while VWP travelers usually do not need a visa to visit this country, they are currently vetted both prior to departure and upon arrival in the United States.

I expect we will discuss that process in more detail at this hearing. Similarly, some are concerned about U.S. citizens who travel to the fight and then seek to return to this country by air. I expect discussion today about what DHS and its Federal partners can do to address such situations, beyond adding individuals to the No-Fly List, if and when the need arises.

Indeed, the Departments of Homeland Security and State play a vital role in disrupting terrorist travel to the United States. This subcommittee has previously examined U.S. visa security and passenger prescreening programs, which are essential to addressing the foreign fighter threat to the homeland.

I hope our DHS and State Department witnesses can speak to us about how these programs operate and how they can be used to address concerns regarding VWP travel specifically. I also hope to hear from our State Department witness about how we are engaging with our foreign partners to help address information gaps regarding individuals of concern and their travel patterns. While the United States cannot resolve the larger situation in Syria and Iraq, we have a responsibility to protect the homeland from threats from ISIL and similar terrorist organizations.

I therefore strongly encourage the administration and Congressional leadership to ensure that all relevant committees, including Intelligence, Armed Services, and Homeland Security, are included in briefings on this matter, so we can work cooperatively to address the various threats posed by ISIL to the United States, both around the world and here in the homeland.

Finally, I look forward to the President's address to the Nation tonight as he outlines his plan for combating ISIL. I remain committed to working with my colleagues on this committee and across Congress to help keep America secure.

Mrs. MILLER. The Chairwoman now recognizes the Ranking Member of the full committee, the gentleman from Mississippi, Mr. Thompson, for his opening statement.

Mr. THOMPSON. Thank you very much, Chairman Miller, Ranking Member Jackson Lee. Thank you for holding today's hearing. I would also like to thank the witnesses for appearing to testify about the Federal Government's efforts to identify foreign fighters in Syria and Iraq who may seek to travel to the United States to do our Nation harm.

Since its establishment in the wake of the terrorist attack of 9/11, this committee has been engaged in helping to address the threats posed by terrorists' travel. For example, Members of the committee advocated for a key provision in the 9/11 Act requiring the implementation of an electronic system for travel authorization to enhance the security of the Visa Waiver Program.

This committee also examined the lessons learned from the attempted bombing of Flight 253 on Christmas day 2009 and urged DHS and the rest of the intelligence community to strengthen programs aimed at identifying and interdicting travelers to this country who might do us harm.

Today, we turn our attention to the threat posed by foreign fighters with Islamic State of Iraq and Lebanon, ISIL, particularly those holding Western passports, who could attempt to travel to this country without obtaining a visa. Top U.S. officials have made public statements warning that Syria-trained extremists, including foreign fighters linked with ISIL, may pose a direct threat to this country. Law enforcement and intelligence officials know that individuals from North America and Europe that travel to Syria could be exposed to radical and extremist influences before returning to their home country.

As Ranking Member Lee has already said, the U.S. Government estimates that there are 12,000 foreign fighters who have traveled to Syria to engage in the on-going civil war, including more than 1,000 Europeans and over 100 U.S. citizens. Of those 100 U.S. citizens fighting in the region, about a dozen are believed to be fighting along ISIL.

I hope our conversation today provides insight into the full scope of foreign fighter issues facing the U.S. Government, as well as how we, along with our foreign partners, can maximize our intelligence and information sharing regarding these individuals. With that in mind, I want to hear from the Department of Homeland Security and Department of State witnesses about their on-going work to identify and interdict foreign fighters coming to the United States, and whether or not they need to increase their efforts in response to ISIL.

We know that the threat posed by ISIL foreign fighters is very real and serious. The American people want assurances that our Government response is and will continue to be equal to the task at hand. Again, I thank the witnesses for joining us today and the Members for holding this hearing.

Madam Chairwoman, with that, I also yield back the balance of my time.

[The statement of Ranking Member Thompson follows:]

STATEMENT OF RANKING MEMBER BENNIE G. THOMPSON

SEPTEMBER 10, 2014

I would like to thank the witnesses for appearing to testify regarding the Federal Government's efforts to identify foreign fighters in Syria and Iraq who may seek to travel to the United States to do our Nation harm. Since its establishment in the wake of the terrorist attacks of 9/11, this committee has been engaged in helping to address the threats posed by terrorist travel. For example, Members of the committee advocated for a key provision in the Implementing 9/11 Commission Recommendations Act of 2007 (Pub. L. 110–53) requiring the implementation of an Electronic System for Travel Authorization to enhance the security of the Visa Waiver Program.

This committee also examined the lessons learned from the attempted bombing of Flight 253 on Christmas day 2009 and urged DHS and its Federal partners to strengthen programs aimed at identifying and interdicting travelers to this country who might do us harm. Today, we turn our attention to the threat posed by foreign fighters with the Islamic State of Iraq and the Levant (ISIL), and particularly those holding Western passports who could attempt to travel to this country without obtaining a visa. Top U.S. officials have made public statements warning that Syria-based extremists, including foreign fighters linked to ISIL, may pose a direct terrorist threat to this country.

U.S. law enforcement and intelligence officials know that individuals from North America and Europe have gone to Syria and will be exposed to radical and extremist influences before possibly returning to their home countries, possibly with intent to do harm. Recent U.S. Government estimates indicate 12,000 foreign fighters have travelled to Syria to engage in the on-going fighting, including more than 1,000 Europeans and over 100 U.S. citizens. Of those 100 U.S. citizens fighting in the region, about a dozen are believed to be with ISIL in particular.

I hope our conversation today provides insight into the full scope of foreign fighter issues facing the U.S. Government as well as how we, along with our foreign partners, can redouble our intelligence, information sharing, and response regarding these individuals. With that in mind, I want to hear from the Department of Homeland Security and Department of State witnesses about their on-going work to identify and interdict foreign fighters coming to the United States, and whether they need to increase their efforts in response to ISIL. We know that the threat posed by ISIL foreign fighters is very real and serious. The American people want assurances that our Government's response is and will continue to be equal to the task at hand.

Mrs. MILLER. I thank the gentleman very much for his opening statement.

I would—before we begin, would ask unanimous consent that a written statement offered by the gentleman from Nevada, Mr. Heck, be included in the record.

Without objection, so ordered.

[The statement of Hon. Heck follows:]

STATEMENT OF HONORABLE JOE HECK

SEPTEMBER 10, 2014

Chairwoman Miller and Ranking Member Jackson Lee: Thank you for allowing me to submit my statement to the record. Like my colleagues that sit on this committee, one of my top priorities as a Member of the House of Representatives is to protect and advance our country's National security efforts.

I am very pleased that the Homeland Security Subcommittee on Border and Maritime Security is having this hearing today to examine the growing threat from ISIL. As we have seen in the media these past few months, the threat from ISIL is very real. They are a violent terrorist organization that threatened our homeland and brutally murdered two of our citizens. Reports indicate that hundreds of ISIS members potentially hold passports from Western allied countries. This is certainly cause for alarm and this committee is right to examine this issue. But what must not get lost in this discussion are the benefits of the Visa Waiver Program (VWP).

As you know, VWP allows citizens from specific countries to travel to the United States for up to 90 days without first obtaining a B1/B2 visa, also known as a tourist visa. Given the name and the way the program facilitates travel to the United States, I understand how one may initially question the role VWP plays in our National security efforts. However, the VWP imposes stringent compliance requirements in order for countries to participate.

Those requirements include:

1. A visa refusal rate below 3%; a condition that must be met before initial designation into VWP.

2. Issuance of International Civil Aviation Organization (ICAO)-compliant electronic passports.

3. Reporting of all lost and stolen passports to the United States via INTERPOL or other means as designated by the Secretary of Homeland Security.

4. Completion of information-sharing agreements with the United States on travelers who may pose a terrorist or criminal threat.

5. Repatriation of criminal aliens.

6. Initial and continuing reviews to determine that a country's VWP designation does not compromise U.S. security, law enforcement, and immigration interests.

7. Independent intelligence assessment of each VWP country in conjunction the previously-mentioned DHS reviews.

Additionally, once a country does become a VWP member, the continual coordination between our intelligence community and of the Members provides constant security assessments that help protect us against potential threats.

The Visa Waiver Program is an effective program that facilitates legitimate travel to the United States while at the same time providing enhanced scrutiny of travelers from participating countries. I understand the concerns that some have, but ultimately preventing a terrorist attack on our homeland is dependent largely upon intelligence sharing with our allies, which the VWP facilitates.

I am eager to review the testimony and the hearing record in the next few days, as well as potential opportunities to further strengthen VWP. Again, thank you Chairwoman Miller and Ranking Member Lee for allowing me to submit my statement. I look forward to working with you on this very important National security program

Mrs. MILLER. Other Members of the committee are reminded that opening statements might be submitted for the record.

Again, we are pleased to have some very distinguished witnesses with us today to discuss this very important topic. Let me more formally introduce them, and then we will just start.

Mr. Troy Miller serves as the acting assistant commissioner for the Office of Intelligence and Investigative Liaison. Mr. Miller and his team are responsible for implementation of intelligence and targeting capabilities, supporting the primary mission of securing America's border by facilitating legitimate travel and trade. Mr. Miller began his career in 1993 as a customs inspector in North Dakota and has since held various positions throughout CBP.

Mr. John Wagner is the assistant commissioner for the Office of Field Operations at the U.S. Customs and Border Protection. Mr. Wagner formerly served as executive director of admissibility and passenger programs with responsibility for all traveler admissibility-related policies and programs.

Ms. Jennifer Lasley is the deputy under secretary for analysis at DHS's Office of Intelligence and Analysis, a position that she has held since April 2013. In this role, Ms. Lasley leads the DHS office charged with providing all-source intelligence analysis of threats to the homeland. Prior to this assignment, she served as vice deputy director for analysis at the Defense Intelligence Agency.

Ms. Hillary Johnson is the acting deputy coordinator for homeland security and multilateral affairs in the State Department's Bureau of Counterterrorism. In this capacity, she oversees whole-of-Government approaches to protecting the homeland on cross-cutting issues such as transportation and cargo security, global supply chain security and terrorism screening and interdictions programs to include terrorism information-sharing negotiations and agreements with foreign partners to combat terrorist travel.

With that, the Chairwoman would recognize Mr. Miller for his testimony.

STATEMENT OF TROY MILLER, ACTING ASSISTANT COMMIS-SIONER, INTELLIGENCE AND INVESTIGATIVE LIAISON, U.S. CUSTOMS AND BORDER PROTECTION, U.S. DEPARTMENT OF HOMELAND SECURITY

Mr. MILLER. Chairwoman Miller, Ranking Member Thompson, Ranking Member Jackson Lee, distinguished Members of the committee, thank you for the opportunity to discuss the role of U.S. Customs and Border Protection in securing the homeland against terrorist threats.

More than a decade after the terrorist attacks on September 11, 2001, terrorists continue to focus on commercial aviation as their primary target of interest. As this committee knows, the Department of Homeland Security, specifically CBP, has been aware of and continues to adjust and align our resources to address the evolving nature of the terrorist threat to the homeland.

CBP capabilities allow us to rapidly leverage information and respond to emerging threats as a part of our intelligence-driven counterterrorism strategy. Of particular concern are those threats that continue to emanate from core al-Qaeda, their affiliates, the Islamic State of Iraq and the Levant, ISIL, as well as other like-minded terrorist organizations from across the globe.

CBP's Office of Intelligence has focused on the growing threat of U.S. citizens and Europeans traveling to the Levant to support terrorist activities and those who then return to the United States or allied countries. This past May, a 22-year-old American citizen blew himself up while detonating a massive truck bomb at a restaurant in northern Syria. In addition, in August, two U.S. citizens were killed near Aleppo, Syria, while fighting for extremist groups.

In order to address this and other emerging threats, CBP's Office of Intelligence provides operational and analytic support to our front-line officers on a daily basis through intelligence-based target rules, situational awareness briefings and tactical intelligence, such as link analysis on known subjects of interest.

CBP, in conjunction with our investigative partners, has long-standing protocols for identifying, examining, and reporting on encounters with persons on the terrorist watch list. As a complement to its ability to identify watch-listed individuals attempting to travel, CBP also takes steps to identify those unknown to the law enforcement and intelligence community for further scrutiny. These efforts occur before departure from the United States, before departure from foreign locations destined to the United States, or upon arrival at U.S. ports of entry.

Through robust information sharing and collaboration, CBP continues to work with our law enforcement and intelligence community partners to enhance its comprehensive intelligence-driven targeting program to detect previously-unknown terrorists and their facilitators. For example, CBP's research and analysis on a recent traveler identified by a partner law enforcement agency suspected of being a Syrian foreign fighter revealed the identity of a new suspect, a co-traveler, which provided previously-unknown information to the investigation and expanded our intelligence framework.

As the foreign fighter threat grows, CBP works in close partnership with Federal law enforcement counterterrorism and intelligence communities, State and local law enforcement, as well as the private sector to counter the threat. In addition, the threat posed by Syrian foreign fighters and ISIL is not limited to the United States. There is a growing international commitment to combatting the shared threat to our security. Staff from the CBP's National Targeting Center and our Intelligence Office interact with our foreign counterparts, including those from the five "I" countries, the Middle East, Europe, and North Africa on almost a daily basis to collaborate on efforts to meet this threat.

Most importantly, CBP intelligence works aggressively to continue to leverage assets and resources across the intelligence community and other Federal partners to communicate, coordinate, and collaborate with our international partners, which enables officers and agents to take the appropriate operational response.

In conclusion, CBP will continue to work closely with the DHS enterprise, the Department of State, the Department of Defense, the intelligence community, and our foreign counterparts to detect and address emerging terrorist threats such as those presented by ISIL and identify and address any and all potential security vulnerabilities.

I appreciate the committee's leadership in providing this opportunity to join my colleagues in speaking on this very serious issue. I look forward to working with the committee on this issue and other matters of urgency and priority. I am happy to answer any questions you may have.

[The joint prepared statement of Mr. Miller, Mr. Wagner, and Ms. Lasley follows:]

JOINT PREPARED STATEMENT OF TROY MILLER, JOHN WAGNER, AND JENNIFER LASLEY

SEPTEMBER 10, 2014

Chairwoman Miller, Ranking Member Jackson Lee, and distinguished Members of the subcommittee, thank you for the opportunity to appear today to discuss U.S. Customs and Border Protection's (CBP) security measures to protect our Nation from the threat of terrorists and terrorist weapons, including threats connected with the Islamic State in Iraq and the Levant. I appreciate the committee's leadership and your commitment to helping ensure the security of the American people. This year, CBP celebrates the 225th anniversary of the establishment of the U.S. Customs Service and the important role it played in the history of our Nation. Since its merger into CBP in 2003, Customs has remained a part of CBP's heritage and a significant presence in the continuation of our mission. Today, CBP serves as the front line in defending America's borders against terrorists and instruments of terror and protects our economic security while facilitating lawful international travel and trade. CBP takes a comprehensive approach to border management and control, combining National security, customs, immigration, and agricultural protection into a coordinated whole.

CBP'S INTELLIGENCE-DRIVEN TRAVEL SECURITY OPERATIONS

As this committee knows, we live in a world of ever-evolving threats. From this perspective, CBP is now focused on the literally thousands of foreign fighters, including U.S. citizens, who continue to gravitate toward Syria to engage in that protracted civil war. Many of these are fighting alongside violent extremist groups both in Syria and in neighboring Iraq, learning battlefield skills and terrorist tradecraft.

Of the numerous insurgent groups active in Iraq, Islamic State of Iraq and al-Sham (ISIS) demonstrated focus on consolidating territory in the Middle East region to establish their own Islamic State is of particular concern. Since June 2014, ISIS (also known as the Islamic State of Iraq and the Levant (ISIL)) and its allies have gained control of Mosul, Iraq's second-largest city, captured significant territory across central Iraq, and continue to engage with Iraqi security forces in that region.

In early August, the threat to the Iraqi Kurdistan Region increased considerably with the advance of ISIL towards Kurdish areas.

As foreign fighters supporting ISIL's regional aggression retain the ability to travel to their countries of origin and beyond, they have the potential to threaten the homeland.[1]

In response to the potential threat posed by ISIL and other terrorist groups seeking to gain access to the homeland, CBP, and more broadly the Department of Homeland Security (DHS), is continually refining our risk-based strategy and layered approach to security, extending our borders outward, and focusing our resources on the greatest risks to interdict threats before they reach the United States. CBP processes nearly 1 million travelers each day at our Nation's ports of entry, and about 30 percent—over 100 million a year—of these travelers arrive via commercial aviation. Given that terrorist organizations primarily seek to use commercial air transportation to move operatives into the United States or as a means to attack the homeland, our testimony will focus on international air travel.

CBP continually evaluates and supplements layered security measures with enhancements to strengthen DHS's ability to identify and prevent the international travel of those individuals or groups that wish to do us harm. The success of targeted security measures depends on the ability to gather, analyze, share, and respond to information in a timely manner—using both strategic intelligence to identify existing and emerging threat streams, and tactical intelligence to perform link analysis and targeted responses.

Our intelligence-driven strategies are integrated into every aspect of our travel security operations. CBP develops and strategically deploys resources to detect, assess, and, if necessary, mitigate the risk posed by travelers at every stage along the international travel sequence—including when an individual applies for U.S. travel documents; reserves, books, or purchases an airline ticket; checks-in at an airport; while en route and upon arrival at a U.S. port of entry.

Safeguards for Visas and Travel Authorization

One of the initial layers of defense in securing international air travel is preventing dangerous persons from obtaining visas, travel authorizations, and boarding passes. Before boarding a flight destined for the United States, most foreign nationals must obtain a non-immigrant visa (NIV)—issued by a U.S. embassy or consulate—or, if they are eligible to travel under the Visa Waiver Program (VWP), they must apply for a travel authorization.

For eligible individuals traveling under the VWP, CBP operates the Electronic System for Travel Authorization (ESTA).[2] ESTA, is a web-based system through which individuals must apply for travel authorization prior to boarding an aircraft destined for the United States. Through ESTA, CBP conducts enhanced vetting of VWP applicants in advance of travel to the United States in order to assess whether they are eligible to travel under the VWP or could pose a risk to the United States or the public at large. Through information-sharing agreements, CBP provides other U.S. Government agencies' ESTA application data for the purpose of helping CBP make a determination about an alien's eligibility to travel without a visa and for law enforcement and administrative purposes. Additionally, CBP requires air carriers to verify that VWP travelers have a valid authorization before boarding an aircraft bound for the United States.

Travelers that require NIVs to travel to the United States must apply to the Department of State (DOS) under specific visa categories depending on the purpose of their travel, including those as visitors for business, pleasure, study, and employment-based purposes. We respectfully refer you to our colleagues in the DOS Bureau of Consular Affairs for additional details about the visa application and adjudication processes.

---

[1] Sources for ISIL background: Reflections on the Tenth Anniversary of *The 9/11 Commission Report, http://bipartisanpolicy.org/library/report/rising-terrorist-threat-9-11-commission*; Transcript/Remarks as Delivered by The Honorable James R. Clapper Director of National Intelligence 9/11 Commission 10th Anniversary Tuesday, July 22, 2014 11:00 a.m.; *http://www.dni.gov/index.php/newsroom/speeches-and-interviews/202-speeches-interviews-2014/1095-remarks-as-delivered-by-dni-clapper-on-the-9-11-commission-10th-anniversary?highlight=WyJ-pc2lsIl0* Iraq Travel Warning, Last Updated: August 10, 2014; *http://travel.state.gov/content/passports/english/alertswarnings/iraq-travel-warning.html*; Airstrikes in Iraq: What You Need to Know *http://www.whitehouse.gov/blog/2014/08/11/airstrikes-iraq-what-you-need-know.*

[2] Exceptions would be citizens of countries under other visa exempt authority, such as Canada. Citizens of countries under visa exempt authority entering the United States via air are subjected to CBP's screening and inspection processes prior to departure. In the land environment, they are subjected to CBP processing upon arrival at a U.S. port of entry.

In an effort to augment and expand traveler targeting operations, Immigration and Customs Enforcement (ICE) has co-located Visa Security Program (VSP) personnel at the National Targeting Center (NTC)—a 24/7 operation where analysts and targeting officers to assess the risk of every international traveler at each stage of the travel continuum, leveraging intelligence materials and law enforcement data. This allows ICE special agents and intelligence analysts to conduct thorough analysis and in-depth investigations of high-risk visa applicants. The focus of the VSP and NTC are complementary: The VSP is focused on identifying terrorists and criminal suspects and preventing them from exploiting the visa process and reaching the United States, while the NTC provides tactical targeting and analytical research in support of preventing terrorist and terrorist weapons from entering the United States. The co-location of VSP personnel at the NTC helps increase both communication and information sharing.

To further enhance traveler screening efforts, ICE, CBP, and DOS are collaborating and have begun to implement an automated visa application screening process that expands significantly DHS' ability to identify serious threats to National security and public safety at the point of inception in an individual's immigration life cycle and revolutionizes the way the U.S. Government screens foreign nationals seeking entry to the United States. The program also results in synchronized reviews of information across these agencies and allows for a unified DHS response and recommendation regarding a visa applicant's eligibility to be issued a visa. The collaborative program leverages the three agencies' expertise, authorities, and technologies, such as CBP's Automated Targeting System (ATS), to screen pre-adjudicated (approved) visa applications. It significantly enhances the U.S. Government's anti-terrorism efforts, improving the existing process by extending our borders outward and denying high-risk applicants the ability to travel to the United States.

In March 2010, the NTC implemented a new program to conduct continuous vetting of U.S. NIVs that have been recently issued, revoked, and/or denied.[3] This recurrent vetting ensures that changes in a traveler's visa status are identified in near-real-time, allowing CBP to immediately determine whether to provide a "no board" recommendation to a carrier or recommend that DOS revoke the visa, or whether additional notification should take place for individuals determined to be within the United States. If a potential visa ineligibility or inadmissibility is discovered for U.S.-bound travelvers, CBP will request that DOS revoke the visa and recommend that the airline not board the passenger. If no imminent travel is identified and derogatory information exists that would render a subject inadmissible, CBP will still coordinate with DOS for a prudential visa revocation. (Note: CBP may recommend that an airline not board a passenger even if the passenger holds a valid visa.) If DOS has revoked, or if CBP has requested revocation of, an individual's visa and the individual is found to be in the United States, CBP will notify the ICE Counterterrorism and Criminal Exploitation Enforcement Unit for enforcement action. Where applicable, CBP will share any derogatory information with U.S. Citizenship and Immigration Services to ensure denial of benefits. Additionally, the DOS Bureau of Diplomatic Security has over 100 special agents embedded in consular sections at 97 U.S. embassies and consulates. These agents have access to derogatory information uncovered by CBP and can work with host country law enforcement officials to conduct local investigations.

Recurrent Vetting

Vetting of passengers and travel information occurrs repeatedly throughout the travel sequence.

CBP gathers information and assesses risk when travel is booked and conducts pre-departure and out-bound screening for all international flights arriving in and departing from the United States by commercial air. When a traveler purchases a ticket for travel to the United States, a passenger name record (PNR) is generated in the airline's reservation system. PNR data may contain information on itinerary, co-travelers, changes to the reservation, and payment information. CBP receives passenger data from commercial air carriers at operationally-determined intervals up to 96 hours prior to departure and concluding at the scheduled departure time.

Further, Advance Passenger Information System (APIS) regulations require that commercial air carriers transmit all passenger and crew manifest information before departure, prior to securing the aircraft doors. CBP vets APIS information, which includes passenger biographic data and travel document information, on all international flights to and from the United States against the Terrorist Screening Data-

---

[3] CBP continually vets against denied NIVs that were denied for National security reasons, but not for all NIV denials.

base (TSDB), criminal history information, records of lost or stolen passports, public health records, and prior immigration or customs violations and visa refusals. CBP uses APIS and PNR data to identify known or suspected threats before they depart the foreign location.

CBP leverages all available advance passenger data including the PNR and APIS data, previous crossing information, intelligence, and law enforcement information, as well as open-source information in its anti-terrorism efforts at the NTC. Starting with the earliest indications of potential travel and continuing through the inspection or arrivals process, the NTC continuously analyzes information using the ATS, a decision-support tool for CBP officers. CBP matches travelers' information against risk-based criteria developed based on actionable intelligence derived from current intelligence community reporting or other law enforcement information available to CBP.

CBP's pre-departure vetting efforts work in concert with Transportation Security Administration's (TSA) Secure Flight program, which vets 100 percent of passengers flying to, from, over, and within the United States, as well as international point-to-point U.S. carriers, against the No-Fly, Selectee, and expanded Selectee portions of the TSDB. Secure Flight provides nearly instant identification of potential matches, allowing for expedited notification of law enforcement, airlines, and our partners in the intelligence community to prevent individuals on the No-Fly list from boarding an aircraft, as well as ensuring that individuals on the TSDB with the "selectee" designation receive appropriate enhanced screening prior to flying. Secure Flight allows TSA, CBP, and our partners in the intelligence community to adapt quickly to new threats by accommodating last-minute changes to the risk categories assigned to individual passengers.

Pre-Departure Programs

CBP's Pre-Departure Targeting Program utilizes a layered enforcement strategy to prevent terrorists and other inadmissible aliens from boarding commercial aircraft bound for the United States. Three key components of the Pre-Departure Targeting Program are the Immigration Advisory Program (IAP), the Joint Security Program (JSP), and the Regional Carrier Liaison Groups (RCLGs). IAP and JSP support the Pre-Departure Targeting Program with IAP/JSP Officers who are posted at 11 foreign airports in the Netherlands, the United Kingdom, Japan, Germany, Spain, France, Qatar, Panama, and Mexico. These IAP/JSP Officers work with the border security agencies of the host country and commercial airlines in order to recommend the denial of boarding to high-risk subjects. The RCLGs, which are located in Honolulu, Miami, and New York, and are staffed by CBP Officers, are responsible for the remaining non-IAP airports around the world. The RCLGs utilize established relationships with the commercial airlines to prevent passengers who may pose a security threat, have fraudulent documents, or are otherwise inadmissible from boarding flights to the United States. In fiscal year 2013, through the Pre-Departure Targeting Program, NTC identified 5,378 passengers who would have been deemed inadmissible to the United States, and coordinated to prevent them from boarding aircraft at foreign locations by providing "no-board" recommendations to carriers.

CBP's Pre-clearance locations in Aruba, Bermuda, the Bahamas, Canada, Ireland, and the United Arab Emirates (UAE) provide another avenue of security by providing for the inspection and clearance of commercial passengers on foreign soil. CBP Officers are in uniform, and have the legal authorities to question travelers and inspect luggage. All mission requirements are completed at the pre-clearance port prior to travel, including immigration, customs, and agriculture inspections. In the UAE, CBP Officers have the greatest authorities of any of our other agreements. The UAE receives flights from Yemen, North and East Africa (Morocco, Nigeria, Kenya, Ethiopia, and Sudan), Saudi Arabia, Pakistan, Iraq, Iran, Lebanon, Bangladesh, and India, all high-risk pathways for terrorist travel. The underlying principle of this pre-clearance agreement is the mitigation of threats, both known and unknown, based on our analysis of current threats. There they are allowed a full complement of authorities to question and search individuals and baggage, access to the full complement of technology systems, and are authorized to have access to firearms and other law enforcement tools. Additionally, ICE, Homeland Security Investigations, has an attaché office located in the U.S. Embassy in Abu Dhabi to follow up on any investigative leads generated from CBP pre-clearance operations.

Arrival Processing

Upon arrival in the United States, all persons are subject to inspection by CBP Officers. CBP Officers scan the traveler's entry documents to perform queries of various CBP databases for exact or possible matches to existing look-outs, including those of other law enforcement agencies. For most foreign nationals arriving at U.S.

airports, CBP Officers collect biometrics—fingerprints and photographs—and compare them to any previously-collected information. Once a verified identity is established, CBP systems will identify any watch list information and return the results to the officer for appropriate processing. In addition to the biographic and biometric system queries performed, a CBP Officer interviews each traveler to determine the purpose and intent of their travel, and whether any further inspection is necessary based on, among other things, National security, admissibility, customs, or agriculture concerns.

Identifying and separating low-risk travelers from those who may require additional scrutiny is a key element in CBP's efforts to facilitate and secure international travel. CBP's trusted traveler programs, such as Global Entry, provide expedited processing upon arrival in the United States for pre-approved, low-risk participants through the use of secure and exclusive lanes and automated kiosks.

Additionally, CBP has established a Counter-Terrorism Response (CTR) protocol at ports of entry for passengers arriving with possible links to terrorism. CTR protocol mandates immediate NTC notification, initiating coordination with the Terrorist Screening Center (TSC), the National Counter Terrorism Center (NCTC), ICE, and the Federal Bureau of Investigation (FBI) Terrorist Screening Operations Unit (TSOU) and National Joint Terrorism Task Force (NJTTF).

Out-bound Operations

In addition to vetting in-bound flights for high-risk travelers, CBP also developed protocols to enhance out-bound targeting efforts within ATS, with the goal of identifying travelers who warrant out-bound inspection or apprehension. Out-bound targeting programs identify potential matches to the TSDB, including potential matches to the "No-Fly" List, as well as National Crime Information Center (NCIC) fugitives, and subjects of active currency, narcotics, and weapons investigations. Additionally, out-bound operations are enhanced by the implementation of targeting rules designed to identify and interdict subjects with a possible nexus to terrorism or links to previously-identified terrorist suspects. As with in-bound targeting rules, out-bound targeting rules are continually adjusted to identify and interdict subjects of interest based on current threat streams and intelligence.

Advance out-bound manifest information is also obtained from carriers through the APIS system. As soon as APIS information becomes available, prior to the departure of a commercial flight, CBP and the TSA immediately begin screening and vetting passengers on the out-bound flight for possible inclusion in the TSDB, including potential matches to the "No-Fly" and Selectee Lists, as well as other law enforcement look-outs.

Programs and Partnerships

CBP's Office of Intelligence and Investigative Liaison (OIIL) serves as the situational awareness hub for CBP and provides timely and relevant information along with actionable intelligence to operators and decision makers. By prioritizing and mitigating emerging threats, risks, and vulnerabilities, OIIL improves CBP's ability to function as an intelligence driven operational organization and turns numerous data points and intelligence into actionable information for analysts and CBP Officers.

CBP works in close partnership with the Federal counterterrorism community, including the FBI, the intelligence community, ICE, TSA, DOS, State and local law enforcement, the private sector, and our foreign counterparts to improve our ability to identify risks as early as possible in the travel continuum, and to implement security protocols for addressing potential threats.

CBP has partnered with the Department of Defense's (DoD) U.S. Special Operations Command (SOCOM) to synchronize planning, authorities, and capabilities to enhance each organization's ability to rapidly and persistently address threats to the homeland before they reach our physical borders. CBP is working with SOCOM components and Theater Special Operations Commands (TSOCs) to develop greater situational awareness of emerging threats, share intelligence, advise on matters of border security, and coordinate enforcement actions as appropriate. CBP and SOCOM–Central Command are working together to leverage each other's capabilities to affect threat networks, such as ISIL, to prevent previously-unknown operational actors and/or facilitators from targeting the homeland.

International Partnerships

As the foreign fighter threat has grown, the international community's response must evolve to keep pace. Nations need appropriate laws, regulations, and enforcement tools and need to take appropriate measures, in coordination with like-minded and transit nations, to help prevent the transit of foreign terrorist fighters across borders and mitigate terrorist recruitment or radicalization to violence. Nations must develop the legal and institutional structures needed to provide international cooperation in the criminal investigation and prosecution of foreign terrorist fighters. International insitutions, such as the United Nations and the International Criminal Police Organization (INTERPOL), must also develop and implement appropriate measures to address this global challenge.

As terrorists change their methods and tactics and technologies continue to evolve, the international community must adapt as quickly as possible. We need to better leverage and coordinate the application of existing tools and structures, strengthen on-going efforts, and facilitate the development of new innovative tools and approaches to preventing and fighting terrorism, while preserving human rights such as freedom of expression. We also need nations to more fully exercise the tools they already have in place to prevent the movement of foreign fighters across their borders.

CONCLUSION

CBP will continue to work with our colleagues within DHS, DOS, FBI, DoD, and the intelligence community to address emerging threats and identify potential security vulnerabilities. In cooperation with other Government agencies and commercial carriers, we will continue to implement our multi-layered defense strategy to secure the aviation sector against terrorists and others who threaten the safety of the traveling public and the security of our Nation.

Chairwoman Miller, Ranking Member Jackson Lee, and Members of the subcommittee, thank you for this opportunity to testify. We look forward to answering your questions.

Mrs. MILLER. Thank you very much.

The Chairwoman recognizes Mr. Wagner for his testimony.

STATEMENT OF JOHN P. WAGNER, ASSISTANT COMMISSIONER, OFFICE OF FIELD OPERATIONS, U.S. CUSTOMS AND BORDER PROTECTION, U.S. DEPARTMENT OF HOMELAND SECURITY

Mr. WAGNER. Thank you, Chairwoman Miller, Ranking Member Thompson, Ranking Member Jackson Lee, distinguished Members of the committee. It is a privilege to appear today to discuss the efforts of U.S. Customs and Border Protection in securing international travel against the threats of terrorists and their supporters.

In response to the potential threat posed by the Islamic State of Iraq and the Levant, other terrorist groups and supporters, including those who are U.S. citizens, CBP and DHS continually refine our border security operations, focusing our resources on the greatest risks and extending our security measures outward to interdict threats before they reach the United States.

Because terrorist organizations continue to primarily target commercial air transportation as a means to move operatives into the United States to attack the homeland, I will focus our operational efforts to detect and respond to the threats in the air environment. Last year, CBP processed over 100 million travelers at our Nation's airports. We have developed and strategically deployed our resources to detect, assess, and mitigate the risk posed by travelers at every stage along the international travel continuum, including when an individual applies for travel documents, reserves or purchases an airline ticket, checks in at the airport, while en route, and upon rival.

Before a foreign national travels to the United States, they are first required to apply for a non-immigrant visa with Department of State or for eligible Visa Waiver Program travelers, a travel authorization from CBP through the Electronic System for Travel Authorization, also known as ESTA.

Before issuing the visa, the Department of State screens each applicant to identify potential risks or ineligibilities. Through ESTA, CBP screens Visa Waiver Program applicants in advance of travel in order to assess eligibility and potential risk to the United States. In this fiscal year, CBP has denied ESTA applications for yearly 300 travelers for security-related reasons.

Now, once travel is booked, but before the flight departs, CBP obtains and analyzes all airline data, including reservation information, also known as PNR, Passenger Name Records, and manifest information, also known as APIS, or Advance Passenger Information, which contains the passport, biographical data, and the flight information, to assess the risk of all passengers, regardless of citizenship or visa status.

CBP's National Targeting Center analyzes traveler data and applies intelligence-driven targeting rules, as just described my by colleague, Mr. Miller, to conduct a risk assessment. If derogatory information or other risks are discovered, CBP is able to take action in several ways overseas prior to actual travel so we can address these concerns.

So in order of descending authorities and capabilities, we have pre-clearance, we have the immigration advisory program, and then we have our regional carrier liaison groups. Our highest capability overseas is pre-clearance, where CBP Officers operate on foreign soil, in uniform, with search authorities and operational capabilities similar to what we have in the United States.

Travelers are questioned, queried through our database, and inspected before they board the aircraft. Pre-clearance requires an agreement with the host country to allow us to operate in such a manner, but after the flight is pre-cleared at a foreign airport, the flight is generally treated as a domestic flight once it arrives in the United States.

There are currently CBP Officers and Agriculture Specialists stationed at 16 locations in six countries. Pre-clearance officers this year have refused entry to 24 travelers for security-related reasons. Our pre-clearance facility in Abu Dhabi, which just opened this year, is of critical importance as it is a transit hub for numerous high-risk pathways for terrorist travel, which gives CBP a critical security operation in a strategic location.

Next is the Immigration Advisory Program, where we have CBP Officers in plain clothes at 11 foreign airports in nine countries to work with air carriers and foreign authorities to work and identify potential threats. They have no search authority per se, but can question travelers in an advisory capacity and can recommend additional security screening or recommend an airline not board a traveler based on the pre-departure vetting I described earlier occurring at our National Targeting Center. So far in this fiscal year, IAP has recommended that foreign airlines deny boarding to over 60 passengers for security-related reasons.

In locations without pre-clearance or IAP operations, we utilize our regional carrier liaison groups that have established relationships with commercial airlines to prevent passengers who may pose a security threat, have fraudulent documents, or are otherwise inadmissible from boarding flights to the United States. These regional carrier liaisons basically are in constant contact with the airlines to exchange this information.

Now at all points in the travel continuum, CBP continues vetting passengers and travel information, including visas and ESTA authorizations, to ensure that any changes in a traveler's eligibility are identified in near-real-time. This continual vetting allows us to coordinate appropriate actions, such as referring individuals for further inspection upon arrival. So far this year, recurrent vetting has caused almost 400 previously-approved ESTAs to be revoked for security-related reasons.

Upon arrival in the United States, all travelers are subject to inspection. Our officers review entry documents, conduct interviews, run appropriate biometric and biographic queries against law enforcement databases. We also have conterterrorism response protocols in place at ports of entry for passengers encountered with possible links to terrorism, which mandates immediate coordination with our National Targeting Center, coordination with our partners at the FBI and the Terrorist Screening Center or the National Counterrorism and ICE.

CBP also conducts out-bound operations, leveraging all available advance travel information and utilizing intelligence-driven targeting rules specific to the out-bound environment to identify, when appropriate, interview, or apprehend travelers for law enforcement or security-related reasons.

So thank you for the opportunity to testify today, and thank you for the attention you are giving to this very important issue. I stand ready to answer any of your questions.

Mrs. MILLER. Thank you very much, Mr. Wagner.

The Chairwoman now recognizes Ms. Lasley.

STATEMENT OF JENNIFER A. LASLEY, DEPUTY UNDER SECRETARY FOR ANALYSIS, OFFICE OF INTELLIGENCE AND ANALYSIS, U.S. DEPARTMENT OF HOMELAND SECURITY

Ms. LASLEY. Thank you, Chairwoman Miller, Ranking Member Thompson, Ranking Member Jackson Lee, and distinguished Members of the committee. I am pleased to be here today with my colleagues from CBP and State Department to discuss the threats to the homeland from foreign fighters traveling to Syria to participate in the conflict there and what we in DHS are doing to mitigate the threats.

As you have correctly stated, the on-going conflict in Syria has emerged as an unprecedented draw for more than 12,000 foreign fighters, including more than 1,000 Europeans and over 100 U.S. persons who have joined or seek to join the fight there. Our concern remains that these individuals, if radicalized, could return to their home countries or to the United States and use their newly-acquired skills to carry out attacks.

We have already seen an example of this in Europe, where in May, a French national who fought alongside the Islamic State of Iraq and the Levant in Syria is charged with conducting a successful attack against a Jewish museum in Brussels, killing 4 people.

Although we currently have no credible information to indicate that the Islamic State of Iraq and the Levant, or ISIL, is planning to attack the homeland, we remain concerned in the long term that their access to Westerners and to safe havens in the Middle East and the Levant will allow them to plan and coordinate attacks in the United States.

More broadly, veteran al-Qaeda fighters have traveled to Syria from Pakistan to take advantage of the permissive operating environment, as well as their easier access to foreign fighters, particularly Europeans and U.S. persons. We are therefore concerned that Syria could emerge as a base of operations for al-Qaeda's international agenda, which could include attacks against the homeland.

We also remain concerned that U.S. persons who link up with violent extremist groups in Syria, regardless of their original reasons for traveling to the country, could gain combat skills, extremist connections and possibly become radicalized or be further persuaded to conduct organized, coordinated, or lone-wolf attacks potentially targeting U.S. and Western interests.

Because DHS border, transportation security, and immigration personnel are at the front lines of many encounters with potential Syrian foreign fighters, the Department is working to ensure that they have the most up-to-date information and can act on it in coordination with law enforcement and ICE partners as appropriate.

I&A is working to inform DHS and State and local law enforcement partners about observable indicators of U.S. persons planning or attempting to travel to Syria. We have produced tailored assessments on the motivations of U.S. travelers, their travel patterns, the role social media is playing in radicalization to violence, and the ways in which U.S. persons are providing material support to Syria-based extremist groups.

We also have partnered with the FBI to produce joint intelligence bulletins and other products for State and local law enforcement on trends in observable behaviors in individuals seeking to travel to Syria to join the fighting. I&A is also partnering with DHS operational components, particularly CBP, TSA, and USCIS, to help identify foreign fighters or other terrorists who may be seeking to travel to the United States, and we are working with international—I am sorry—interagency partners to disrupt their travel or take appropriate law enforcement steps.

We work every day to leverage our unique DHS data to ensure that individuals who are not fully identified in intelligence channels can be appropriately watch-listed and denied entry into the United States.

Finally, we work hand-in-glove with the Department to provide intelligence assessments that support the Visa Waiver Program, a program that DHS has managed since 2003 in consultation with State Department, that facilitates low-risk travelers into the United States for tourism and business. Countries participating in this program must undergo a rigorous review process and agree to share terrorist and criminal information with the United States.

Our intelligence assessments, which are one factor in the country reviews, look at a number of criteria for determining a country's eligibility to participate in the Visa Waiver Program, including the terrorist threat to the United States posed by nationals of that country, the counterterrorism capabilities of that country, the state of information sharing between the U.S. Government and that country, and the security of passports and other identity documents. Using similar criteria, we participate in DHS-led reviews of all Visa Waiver Program countries, which must occur at a minimum every 2 years to evaluate whether a country should remain in the program.

These are just a few of the ways in which we are working to keep the homeland safe from terrorism threats and those posed by returning foreign fighters. Thank you very much for the opportunity to speak with you today about these important issues, and I look forward to your questions.

Mrs. MILLER. Thank you very much.

The Chairwoman now recognizes Ms. Johnson for her testimony.

STATEMENT OF HILLARY BATJER JOHNSON, ACTING DEPUTY COORDINATOR, HOMELAND SECURITY AND MULTILATERAL AFFAIRS, BUREAU OF COUNTERTERRORISM, U.S. DEPARTMENT OF STATE

Ms. JOHNSON. Thank you. Chairwoman Miller, Ranking Member Thompson, Ranking Member Jackson Lee, and distinguished Members of the subcommittee, thank you for the opportunity to appear today on behalf of the State Department and with my colleagues from the Department of Homeland Security or DHS.

We are very deeply supportive of DHS's efforts to protect the U.S. homeland, and we make every effort to amplify its work through diplomatic engagement with our allies and partners. We remain gravely concerned by the activities of terrorists in Syria and Iraq, including the Islamic State Iraq and the Levant, or ISIL, and al-Nusra Front. We have seen in Syria a trend of foreign fighter travel for the purposes of participating in the conflict, largely driven by global connectedness through the internet and social media, on an unprecedented scale. So we at the State Department are working closely with countries affected by the foreign fighter problem to counter the threat these fighters pose.

The Department of State works closely with DHS to support its mission in protecting the United States by promoting effective border security screening with our foreign partners through enhanced information sharing. For example, we believe it is in our best interests to share terrorism screening information with select foreign governments, as all of us face a global terrorist threat that does not recognize National boundaries. To this end, we work closely with the terrorist screening center, which implements information-sharing agreements with foreign partners, including Visa Waiver Program countries. These agreements allow partners to conduct name checks for incoming flights to their countries, which helps us to deter terrorist travel and creates an extra layer of security for the United States.

We also work closely with our partners at DHS to strengthen global aviation security by engaging foreign partners to bolster aviation screening at last points of departure airports with direct flights to the United States. We do this to identify and prevent known or suspected terrorists from boarding commercial flights and to prevent terrorist attacks against global aviation.

Additionally, the Department of State is leading interagency efforts to engage with foreign partners to prevent and interdict foreign extremist travel to Syria, and we work closely with the interagency, including DHS, to expedite comprehensive approaches. This work includes facilitating information exchanges with foreign partners, building partner capacity, and developing shared objectives.

Ambassador Robert Bradtke, senior adviser for partner engagement on Syria foreign fighters, leads this work for the State Department and has met with officials from the European Union member countries, North Africa, the Gulf, the Balkans, and East Asian Pacific to discuss and examine our shared concerns about this threat. Important progress has been made, but more work remains.

Countries in the Balkans have recently adopted or are considering more comprehensive counterterrorism laws. In the Gulf, countries such as Kuwait, Qatar, and Saudi Arabia have increased penalties related to terrorist financing. Several have established the necessary architecture to enforce their counterterrorism laws more effectively.

The European Council recently called for the accelerated implementation of E.U. measures in support of member states to combat foreign fighters. This includes finalizing an E.U. passenger name record, or PNR, as we have mentioned here today, proposal by the end of this year and increasing cooperation with partner nations such as the United States to strengthen border and aviation security in the region.

We will continue to work closely with partners in the coming months to enhance this cooperation and build on our efforts to date. In the week of September 24, President Obama will chair a United Nations Security Council summit on the rising threat posed by foreign terrorist fighters. This presents a unique opportunity to demonstrate the breadth of international consensus and concern regarding the foreign terrorist fighter threat and to build momentum for policy initiatives on this topic at home and abroad.

That same week, Secretary Kerry and the Turkish foreign minister will co-chair a Global Counterterrorism Forum, or GCTF, ministerial meeting. At this meeting, GCTF members will adopt the first-ever set of global good practices to address the foreign terrorist fighter threat. GCTF members will also launch a working group dedicated to working globally to mobilize resources and expertise to advance implementation of these good practices.

In conclusion, the Department of State remains deeply supportive of DHS's efforts to protect the U.S. homeland and make every effort to support its work through our diplomatic engagement efforts. This is a critical component to combatting terrorist travel.

I look forward to answering your questions and working closely with you and our friends and allies across the globe to make the United States safer. Thank you.

[The prepared statement of Ms. Johnson follows:]

PREPARED STATEMENT OF HILLARY BATJER JOHNSON

SEPTEMBER 10, 2014

Chairwoman Miller, Ranking Member Jackson Lee, and distinguished Members of the subcommittee, thank you for the opportunity to appear today on behalf of the State Department with my colleagues from the Department of Homeland Security (DHS). We are deeply supportive of DHS' efforts to protect the U.S. homeland and make every effort to amplify its work through diplomatic engagement and information sharing with our allies and partners.

We remain gravely concerned by the activities of terrorists in Syria and Iraq, including the Islamic State of Iraq and the Levant (ISIL) and al-Nusrah Front. ISIL is an extremely dangerous organization operating in a chaotic part of the world. It has exploited the conflict in Syria and sectarian tensions in Iraq to entrench itself in both countries, now spanning the geographic center of the Middle East. ISIL's attacks in Iraq and Syria have resulted in the deaths of thousands of people and the displacement of hundreds of thousands more from their ancestral homelands. ISIL has brutally targeted all groups who do not fit their narrow world view including some Sunnis, Shia, and religious and ethnic minority groups. In Syria, as in Iraq, ISIL has committed wide-spread atrocities, including torture, murder, the taking and execution of detainees, and hostages sexual violence, and forcible displacement.

We have seen in Syria a trend of foreign fighter travel for the purposes of participating in the conflict—largely driven on an unprecedented scale by global connectivity that is available through the internet and social media. ISIL operates an extremely sophisticated propaganda machine and disseminates timely, high-quality media content on multiple platforms, including on social media. We have seen ISIL use a range of media to attempt to aggrandize its military capabilities, including showcasing the executions of captured soldiers, and evidence of consecutive battlefield victories resulting in territorial gains. More recently, the group's supporters have sustained this momentum on social media by encouraging attacks in the United States and against U.S. interests in retaliation for our air strikes. ISIL has also used its propaganda campaign to draw foreign fighters to the group, including many from Western countries.

It is difficult to provide a precise figure of the total number of foreign fighters in Syria, though the best available estimates indicate that approximately 12,000 fighters from at least 50 countries—including over 100 U.S. persons—may have traveled to Syria to fight for ISIL or al-Nusrah Front since the beginning of the conflict. These fighters not only exacerbate regional instability, but create real threats to U.S. interests and our allies. We are working closely with countries affected by the foreign fighter problem set to counter the threat these fighters pose. As we have built a common picture of the threat with our allies, so, too, we continue our efforts to build consensus around joint initiatives and complementary approaches to sustain a broad and comprehensive approach.

SECURING U.S. BORDERS

The Department of State works closely with the Department of Homeland Security to support its mission in protecting the United States by promoting effective aviation and border security screening with our foreign partners through enhanced information sharing. For example, an important effort in our counterterrorism work is Homeland Security Presidential Directive Six (HSPD–6), a post-9/11 White House initiative. Through HSPD–6, the State Department works with the Terrorist Screening Center to negotiate the exchange of identities of known or suspected terrorists with foreign partners to enhance our mutual border screening efforts.

The Terrorist Screening Center implements these agreements with foreign partners. These agreements allow partners to name-check incoming flights to their countries, which helps us deter terrorist travel, creating an extra layer of security for the United States.

HSPD–6 agreements or arrangements are a pre-requisite to participate in the Visa Waiver Program (VWP). To date, we have 43 such agreements in place which includes VWP partners, and we continue to actively seek out new partners.

The Department of State also works closely with its partners at the Department of Homeland Security to strengthen global aviation security by engaging foreign partners in bolstering aviation screening at last point of departure (LPD) airports with direct flights to the United States to identify and prevent known or suspected terrorists from boarding commercial flights.

FOREIGN TERRORIST FIGHTERS

Additionally, the Department of State is leading interagency efforts to engage with foreign partners to prevent in the first place and, where possible, to interdict foreign extremist travel to Syria. We strongly believe that a whole-of-Government approach is the only way to truly address the threat, and we work closely with our interagency colleagues to facilitate comprehensive approaches. This work includes facilitating information exchanges with foreign partners, building partner capacity, and developing shared objectives focused on addressing the foreign fighter threat. Ambassador Robert Bradtke, Senior Advisor for Partner Engagement on Syria Foreign Fighters, leads this work for the State Department and has met with officials from European Union member countries, North Africa, the Gulf, the Balkans, and East Asia and Pacific, to discuss and examine our shared serious concerns about the foreign terrorist fighter threat. Ambassador Bradtke and other Department counterparts have led sustained efforts to urge reform and build capacity for whole-of-Government and whole-of-society approaches to counter this threat, notably encouraging information sharing and border security, legal reform and criminal justice, and countering violent extremism.

Important progress has been made, but more work remains. Countries in the Balkans recently have adopted or are considering more comprehensive counterterrorism laws. In the Gulf, countries such as Kuwait, Qatar, and Saudi Arabia have increased penalties related to terrorist financing and several have established the necessary architecture to enforce their counterterrorism laws more effectively, such as Kuwait's newly-created Financial Intelligence Unit and Qatar's establishment of a charity abuse review board.

Some of our partners have implemented legal reforms aimed more directly at countering foreign terrorist fighters. For example, traveling overseas to participate in combat has been newly criminalized in the Balkans, Canada, and Jordan. The United Kingdom and Indonesia have banned participation in groups such as ISIL, while Malaysia has publicly opposed ISIL and its activities.

Countries have taken a variety of steps under existing laws and regulations to inhibit foreign fighter's resources or travel. Canada, New Zealand, Australia, and eight European countries have the authority to revoke the passports of suspected foreign fighters.

The European Council recently called for the accelerated implementation of E.U. measures in support of Member States to combat foreign fighters, including finalizing an E.U. Passenger Name Record (PNR) proposal by the end of this year, and increasing cooperation with partner nations such as the United States to strengthen border and aviation security in the region.

In all our efforts with our partners, we stress the importance of—and facilitate implementation of—adhering to a rule of law framework. We are encouraged by these and other reforms to counter the foreign fighter threat. While we have seen progress, our efforts must be sustained and intensified. We will continue to work closely with partners, particularly those in the Middle East, North Africa, and Europe in the coming months to enhance cooperation and build on efforts to date.

MULTILATERAL INITIATIVES AND THE GLOBAL COUNTERTERRORISM FORUM

We are also working the foreign terrorist fighter issue actively on the multilateral front. The week of September 24, President Obama will chair a United Nations Security Council (UNSC) Summit on the rising threat posed by foreign terrorist fighters, no matter their religious ideology or country of origin. This rare UNSC leader-level session is the first U.S.-hosted Head of Government-level UNSC session since President Obama led a UNSC Summit on non-proliferation in September 2009, and it presents a unique opportunity to demonstrate the breadth of international consensus regarding the foreign terrorist fighter threat and to build momentum for policy initiatives on this topic at home and abroad. In addition to a briefing from U.N. Secretary-General Ban Ki-Moon and brief remarks from leaders of all 15 UNSC members, this summit is expected to adopt a U.S.-drafted UNSC Resolution during the session.

That same week, Secretary Kerry and Turkish Foreign Minister Cavusoglu will co-chair a Global Counterterrorism Forum (GCTF) ministerial meeting, where GCTF members will adopt the first-ever set of global good practices to address the foreign terrorist fighter threat (FTF) and launch a working group dedicated to working with GCTF members and non-members alike to mobilize resources and expertise to advance their implementation. The good practices cover the four central aspects of the phenomenon: (1) Radicalizing to violent extremism; (2) recruitment and facilitation; (3) travel and fighting; and, (4) return and reintegration. They are also intended to shape bilateral or multilateral technical or other capacity-building assistance that is provided in this area. This effort will allow our practitioners and other experts to continue to share expertise and broaden skills in addressing the FTF challenge.

CONCLUSION

We remain deeply supportive of DHS's efforts to protect the U.S. homeland and make every effort to support its work through diplomatic engagement.

The State Department is involved in an array of activities to counter terrorism and the phenomenon of foreign terrorist fighters, such as capacity building, countering terrorist finance, and countering violent extremism, my State Department colleagues would be happy to brief Congress about these lines of effort at another time.

Our terrorist adversaries are nimble, and given the vitally important imperative to protect the United States and to stay "one step ahead," we should ensure that the tools of civilian power continue to adapt to serve National security. As I hope you will agree, we have focused and sharpened our efforts, but there remains much to do.

I look forward to answering your questions and working closely with you in making the United States safer, in conjunction with our friends and allies across the globe.

Mrs. MILLER. Thank you all very much.

This subcommittee—and our full committee, but certainly on our subcommittee—has had a number of hearings about visas, about our visas, about the status of our visa programs. We certainly have had a lot of discussion about the Visa Waiver Program in a hearing that we had a year ago this month, in a hearing in March of this year. This subcommittee has asked a lot of questions about the Visa Waiver Program, and so we certainly understand that the program started back in the mid-1980s really to expedite tourism and travel, which was a very good idea at that time.

But the world is changing. As we think about things that we need to do to grow our economy, we also have to consider some of these various processes and systems that we have in place with other countries, our allies, our friends, and what kinds of programs we have actually put in place that put America at risk.

So to that, I guess my first question would be—we have heard a lot of testimony here today and even in our opening statements about estimates as many as 12,000 foreign fighters coming from so many European countries that can travel Western passports that are in the visa—some countries that are in the waiver program, et cetera. One of the things, obviously, in the Visa Waiver Program requires information sharing.

As we sit here on the day before—we are talking about 9/11, really—one of the things that the 9/11 commission recommendations—a recommendation that they made—an observation that they made that always sticks in my mind is how we had to move, really, from the need-to-know information to the need-to-share information.

Information sharing is such a critical component to be a country that is participating in the Visa Waiver Program here with the United States. We certainly see, for instance, the passenger name record, the PNR data, which we can utilize to identify fighters or suspicious travelers or what have you, we see our ally, as I mentioned in my opening statement, the United Kingdom being so great on sharing information. Everybody gives them accolades for their sharing of information with us.

But some of the other European countries may be not so good. Even in our own hemisphere, it appears that Mexico is pretty good. At least I have heard that. Canada—there have been some concerns raised about information sharing there.

I guess I would say, first of all, how many countries do we currently have? I think it is close to 30. Are there any that have ever been eliminated from this program? Are there any that we are thinking about? Are there things that the agencies are able to do to really be much more aggressive about making sure that we are getting the information that we think we need shared with us, in order for these—the countries to participate in the visa waiver? Are there things that we need to be doing legislatively to assist the agencies?

I am not quite sure who I am directing this question to. Who would like to start with that, Mr. Wagner, Ms. Lasley? Yes.

Ms. LASLEY. I can certainly give you a little bit of background in terms of how many members we have today in the Visa Waiver Program. So currently, we have 38 members, 30 from Europe, 7 from the Asia-Pacific region, and 1 in Latin America.

It is my understanding that we have—since the inception of the program, as you—as you stated, in the 1980s, two countries have been taken from the Visa Waiver Program list. That was Argentina and Uruguay. But it was many years ago, and it was not because of terrorism-related issues but more economic issues.

Mrs. MILLER. Is there any thought about—as I say, is there anything that you need from us legislatively to assist you in being more aggressive about—I mean, if there are these kinds of concerns about information sharing from any of these countries, should we be much more aggressive about the information that we think we need in order to feel comfortable to continue to have visa waiver eligibility from these various countries?

Mr. WAGNER. So we do get a lot of information from these countries. You know, we do—they do sign the information-sharing agreements. We do do the biennial—every-2-year review of the countries and their procedures. They do report their lost and stolen passports. Then all the travelers do fill out the ESTA application, where we get about 17 data elements, which we run through a series of background checks, and then the recurring checks, some of the numbers I mentioned earlier.

You know, we denied this fiscal year, which is coming to close in a couple weeks, 285 ESTA applications for security reasons. We have revoked 393. This was after it was issued. When we do our recurring vetting, new information had come to light that caused us to issue that revocation. Our total applications we have denied this year is over 35,000. So it is a small number of the overall denials, but yes, a very consequential and important number.

So some of the things we are looking at is reviewing all of our procedures, our data collection efforts. Are we getting the right data elements? Are there other elements we need? Are there other elements we can use? You know, how does it impact, you know, the privacy of individuals? How does it impact our travel and tourism facilitation efforts, as well? You know, what would we do with the data if we collected it? But these are the things we are reviewing, along with many other—our other procedures and things we continue to do in all of our programs.

Mrs. MILLER. Following up on that, we talk about the ESTA, which stands for the Electronic System for Travel Authorization, as you know, was added as a security requirement actually by Congress after 9/11. Previous to that, we didn't have—we didn't have the ESTA. As you mentioned, 17 different elements that you are asking on the form, Mr. Wagner—the name, obviously, the name, passport number, et cetera, et cetera, information elements that you are obtaining that you can then check against our databases, et cetera.

But the full visa application, you have to have about 110 pieces of information apparently that are required. In regards to the ESTA—and I was taking some notes when you were saying here about the ESTAs that have been revoked and denied, et cetera.

I actually am drafting some legislation right now, and I guess this is one of the things I am going to ask you here. I am drafting legislation currently, hope to be introduced perhaps even today, that we would clarify what the purpose of ESTA actually is, that we need to ensure that terrorists don't get on airplanes, and then asking the Department to tell us what other changes to ESTA may be necessary to increase security.

So I am again asking you, I guess, for your—what your thought is on legislation like that. Do you think the agencies, again, have the authority, short of any Congressional legislation, to ask for additional—it would seem to me—I am not in your business, but it would seem to me that asking for additional information, particularly from a number of these countries that are in the Visa Waiver Program, more than just the 15 or 17 pieces of information would be something that would be under consideration.

Again, do you think you have the authority to do that, understanding that ESTA was initiated, again, by the Congress after 9/11, after the commission from their recommendations, and should we be giving you legislation to assist you there?

Mr. WAGNER. Thank you. We are reviewing this, as well as a number of other programs that we have. I—part of that review is: Do we need additional authorities to collect additional information? I believe in ESTA, we have—I believe we have the authorities, but that is one of the things we are reviewing, what other types of information would we need? Could we use it? How would we use it? How would we collect it? Is it verifiable information? Is it useful information? Do we have systems to actually make use of that data that we would collect, and would it be helpful?

So we are looking at those things. As an operational organization, we are always looking for additional data and additional data sources, but again, with respect to people's privacy, and you know—is there a useful need for us to collect that information, and can we actually put it to use?

But you know, in general, as coupled with the PNR and the airline data, it really helps us paint a better picture of travelers and where they are going, for how long, and what other information we can relate that to. So having, in general terms, a broader set of data to allow us to identify individuals or even identify individuals who are not the person we are looking for because we have the additional data and we can dismiss any connections we may think are there with the person, so—but that is one of the things, balancing the privacy and the costs and where we would keep the information.

Mrs. MILLER. Just being cognizant certainly of my time here, but I am going to ask one other additional question, and think about this a bit, because in addition to that piece of legislation, I am also preparing a piece of legislation that would seek to clarify the authorization that I think the Department of State already has, in order to revoke passports. We are looking at what Cameron is doing in the United Kingdom certainly and with dual citizenship, et cetera.

Again, we are a very free and open society, but we are living in a changing world here. Whether or not you have the authorization to revoke these passports—how can we help you clarify that? Because I was looking through the—trying to become familiar with exactly what has to happen to lose your citizenship.

For instance, it talks about if you are entering or serving in the armed forces of a foreign state. So perhaps that is ambiguous a bit when we are talking about terrorist organizations because they are not really a foreign state. These are the kinds of things that I think this committee is looking for today from you. We want to give you the tools that you need to help you to protect the homeland. If there is a flaw in what we have, it is not strong enough, we need to get that kind of feedback from all of you.

I don't know if anyone has any comment on that before I go to the next Member.

Ms. JOHNSON. Just briefly, the State Department does have the authority to revoke passports on National security grounds. We are very concerned, as you know, about the over 100 Americans that are in the foreign fighter ranks.

We do work with—very closely with our law enforcement and intelligence partners on information because we don't just unilaterally revoke passports, of course. But this is a consular affairs bureau issue set. So we are reviewing right now in consultation with our law enforcement and intelligence partners our current tools at our disposals and authorities because this is a big concern, that we want to look to be able to use that authority if we need it, but not interrupt legitimate travel of other U.S. citizens who are constructively engaged in the region.

Mrs. MILLER. I appreciate that. I would just mention that time is of the essence here, I think. I think you can see that because of the consternation on behalf of the American people of this. So this is not an issue we just sort of want to go off there infinitum. I think you are going to be looking at some—as I say, I am one Member that is going to be introducing legislation today about these issues. I am trying to assist you, and you know, we will see how quickly the Congress can actually act. But we are looking for feedback from all of you.

With that, the Chairwoman recognizes the Ranking Member, Ms. Jackson Lee from Texas.

Ms. JACKSON LEE. Again, let me thank the Chairman and thank my Ranking Member, and as well, the Chairman of the full committee. Again, this hearing is not to draw you over here to the

United States House as much as it is to make an important statement of oversight to act.

I started my remarks by saying that in the—and on the eve of 9/11, and although there has been much commentary of the potential threat that ISIL poses, I am not willing to cede the point and agree to those who have a perspective that the United States may not be in the eye of the storm.

I think the way we respond to it is experienced and balanced and sure as it relates to providing security for our citizens. I thank you all for being on the front lines of doing that. That is what the Department was created for, and that is what the committee is created for, as well.

So I want to go to a pointed question. In the collaboration between State and the Department of Homeland Security in particular, intelligence, and dealing with CBP, is it your thought that the ISIL actions in Syria and Iraq and the ISIL profile could be a threat to the United States? Mr. Miller.

Mr. MILLER. Yes, ma'am. With as you stated, over 100 Americans that have traveled to fight with ISIL and Nusra Front and other extremist groups overseas, plus—and Western Europeans, I do believe that it could be a short-term and a long-term threat to the United States.

Ms. JACKSON LEE. Mr. Wagner.

Mr. WAGNER. Yes, I also agree. You know, looking at the systems we have and how we look at, you know, the information we get from the airlines with a person's reservation information and looking at their itineraries and other characteristics of their travel, you know, do they fit what we know about, you know, what the intelligence reporting are known factors?

Are these—are we identifying individuals that then we want to have a further inspection with and try to—you know, to talk to them and try to determine what their purpose and their intent of travel is.

We have good systems to be able to do that. We have good intelligence reporting to help us build those characteristics we are looking for, and we get good information from Department of State and other entities. When we do want to take actions against known individuals, then we have the systems in place to identify them and figure out what point in that process we need to intercept them and have that discussion.

Ms. JACKSON LEE. Ms. Lasley.

Ms. LASLEY. Ma'am, we certainly assess that ISIL presents a long-term threat to the country. We know that their leader back in January spoke of a direct confrontation with the United States. As I said, we don't see a near-term threat directly from them, no evidence yet of that. But they do have a very sophisticated and savvy media campaign, especially a social media campaign. I think our near-term concern is that that campaign will be quite appealing to individuals who would seek to radicalize, whether they are over in Europe or they are here in the homeland. They could conduct an attack on their own at any time, based on that media campaign. So that is a very clear near-term concern that we have.

Ms. JACKSON LEE. Ms. Johnson.

Ms. JOHNSON. We would echo all of those comments. I think for both the State Department, it is not just the homeland, but our U.S. citizens overseas. So we are also looking at that aspect. We know ISIL's stated threats and objectives against the United States. So we look at our protection of our U.S. citizens overseas, as well as our missions and are always adjusting our posture accordingly.

Ms. JACKSON LEE. Let me ask a specific question. Thank you. As both Mr. Miller and Mr. Wagner knows, and as we all know, the two acts of beheading were clearly directed toward the sentiments, the infrastructure values of the United States, and certainly, as Ms. Johnson has said, attack on our citizens that were overseas.

To Mr. Miller and Mr. Wagner: Following upon the line of questioning of Chairwoman Miller, I am concerned as to whether or not we do have the kind of coordination that is actually needed. I guess I don't want to use the term "imminent." I think creating hysteria is not the intent of this committee.

But I also hesitate to be able to solidly predict ISIL's threat level, inasmuch as we are reminded of our posture on the day before 9/11, 2001. So let me just—in the manner in which you can answer the question, feel comfortable about the level of coordination in this climate.

Mr. Miller, I would like to hear what level, how intense your coordination is, how comfortable you are with the coordination. What do you need to make it better? I would ask Mr. Wagner that question.

Mr. MILLER. Our coordination with the intelligence community and the law enforcement community in the United States is stronger than ever. We are working this threat daily, whether it is with the FBI and the intelligence community.

Our foreign counterparts—we are working with them. I just met with the Australians and the United Kingdom yesterday. There is stronger and stronger sentiment for information sharing from our European partners, as well. We can explain some of our relationships, burgeoning relationships in a Classified environment more fully.

Ms. JACKSON LEE. Mr. Wagner.

Mr. WAGNER. We take that information and we make operational decisions based upon it. Getting that information is really critical to us making the right decisions on how we operationalize that information.

One of the things, you know, we would like to see is a stronger response from some of our partners overseas and emulating some of the ways we do our border security management, as was referenced earlier, you know, use of PNR and use of the airline manifest information in trying to take actions in advance of travel and not waiting until that person shows up on your doorstep to figure out what to do with them.

I think we would encourage all of our allies around the globe to consider those types of systems and those practices. We work very closely with a lot of countries in helping build up that capacity.

Ms. JACKSON LEE. I have about two questions, if I might, just finish very quickly. Ms. Johnson, I understand that it is somewhat difficult to track the travel of foreign terrorists. I would like to know what the State Department is doing and how you are improving tracking the travels of foreign terrorists and coordinating with your fellow collaborating nation-states about whether you are doing that.

Ms. Lasley, if I can ask you the question of our level of intelligence in the climate of what we are in now, and backtrack it to 9/11, where we were saying quite the contrary. We didn't have a slight inkling of what was going to be happening that next day. Are we in a better place, and is there something more that you need? Ms. Johnson.

Ms. JOHNSON. Thank you. Obviously, working with our foreign partners is an on-going effort. Everyone has different legal regimes and privacy concerns, but they are very concerned—our foreign partners are very concerned about the foreign fighter terrorist threat, and we are working with them very closely. As I mentioned, the European is now looking at the Passenger Name Record situation, hoping to adopt something by the end of this year. That will help us at the United States for the CBP Officers to be able to understand who is coming and who is traveling. We are——

Ms. JACKSON LEE. Do you think the No-Fly List can be made more robust?

Ms. JOHNSON. The No-Fly List?

Ms. JACKSON LEE. Yes, make it more robust?

Ms. JOHNSON. I think for the No-Fly List, I think we are working very—all the time talking about how to we can work the No-Fly List to make sure it has got accurate information, that is it is operational. We do share that information with foreign partners so they know who is on the No-Fly List. We have worked on aviation screening generally with our foreign partners, particularly last point of departure airports. They are enhancing their own screening efforts. That helps us prevent people from even getting on planes, including from other parts of the world to our European allies' airports.

As I mentioned, our information-sharing agreements, particularly with the visa waiver partner countries, but also additional countries under Homeland Security Presidential Directive 6. We share biographic information with foreign partners. A lot of that information, again, is individuals on the No-Fly List and those who need to be more screened.

We also have something I think that DHS and DOJ can talk about, the preventing serious crime agreements, which also collects biographic—or I am sorry, biometric information, mostly fingerprints—to exchange that information. So there are a lot of capabilities there to enhance our border security screening and track terrorist travel.

Mrs. MILLER. I am going to ask in the interests of time here—we are way over the time here—that Ms. Lasley answer her question in writing.

The Chairwoman now recognizes the gentleman—the Ranking Member, Mr. Thompson.

Mr. THOMPSON. Thank you very much, Madam Chairwoman. Mr. Wagner, from time to time, Congress has in its infinite wisdom cut the budget of the agencies who are tasked on the front line to keep us safe. In the present budget, are you comfortable that you can provide the security and assurance necessary that CBP is doing all it can to keep bad people from getting into the country?

Mr. WAGNER. Yes, I believe we can. I think CBP was fortunate enough to, you know, be one of the few organizations that did see a very generous budget, including the addition of 2,000 CBP Officers this fiscal year. In the administration's request for 2015, there is also a request for another 2,000-plus officers, which we know are critically important to securing the economy, but also then securing and facilitating—securing and countering this threat.

Mr. THOMPSON. I understand the manpower. But I am concerned about technology and some other things necessary to support the increase in people along the border. I am looking at the international side of it.

Mr. WAGNER. Well, we use those officers to deploy them in places like pre-clearance overseas, deploy them in our immigration advisory program, deploy them to our National Targeting Center, to be able to—when we collect the information, we collect the intelligence reports and operationalize that, it is CBP Officers and analysts and others, too, but principally CBP Officers, based on their experience and their knowledge in turning that into actionable operational entities and being able to question these travelers at different points in their travel continuum to address that.

Mr. THOMPSON. So it is not a matter of resources. So are you satisfied with the coordination between the agencies in terms of identifying these individuals coming to this country?

Mr. WAGNER. Yes. I think we have seen that it has been better than ever at this point. As these threats continue to—you know, to appear, you know, the information sharing and the coordination get stronger and stronger, and you know, our systems integration to make sure our databases are talking to each other. So when State Department takes an action against a visa or a passport, it appears in our database so we can take action when that traveler tries to travel or begins their travel.

Mr. THOMPSON. Let's take that example. Is that a real-time identification, or is there lag time?

Mr. WAGNER. It would be a real-time identification that that information appears in the different systems, and then we try to access it in—far in advance of a person's travel as we can in order to take the appropriate action or to address whatever kind of questions we have. So yes.

Mr. THOMPSON. Ms. Johnson, there has been some discussion about revoking of passports. For the committee's edification, are the present rules for revoking passports as robust as they need to be, given this present ISIS threat that potentially is expanding?

Ms. JOHNSON. Thank you. I know our consular affairs bureau is working with our law enforcement and intelligence community partners to review all of our options, and I believe they are looking at that, as well. I can take that back to have our lawyers and the consular affairs bureau provide a more fulsome answer, if you would like.

Mr. THOMPSON. Well, I would. But if you would, are you comfortable, with the present protocols in place that if those individuals are identified, that the passport cancellation process would fully comply with that cancellation?

Ms. JOHNSON. I think that is a question that consular affairs bureau could answer better. But I believe it is in real time. When we revoke passports, I believe—I don't know how many we have done—that it is pretty quick. But again, we do it in consultation with the law enforcement and the intelligence communities so there should be operational activities working side-by-side on that very quickly, I imagine.

Mr. THOMPSON. Can anybody else address that question? Well, can you get Consular Affairs to provide it? I think one of the questions that we are contemplating is whether or not, when these individuals are identified, that we are doing everything we can to keep them from getting back here to American soil. If there is some question as to whether or not that is, in fact, taking place, we need to plug any potential gap that exists.

I yield back, Madam Chairwoman.

Mrs. MILLER. I thank the gentleman very much.

The Chairwoman now recognizes the Chairman of the full committee, the gentleman from Texas, Chairman McCaul.

Chairman MCCAUL. I thank you, Madam Chairwoman, for holding this important hearing, very timely. I thank you for your leadership, as well.

Tomorrow, we will observe the 13th anniversary of the 9/11 terrorist attacks. While we have made a tremendous amount of progress since that tragic day in 2001, we have to continue to be vigilant and be one step ahead of our adversaries. Today, ISIS is the biggest threat to the homeland. These terrorists are brutal, driven, and intent on attacking the United States.

The job of this committee is to help ensure that this does not happen. The largest concern is ISIS's recruitment of foreign fighters, many of whom have Western passports that could ease their travel into Europe and into the United States to carry out attacks. The fact is, you don't know what you don't know, and we only have estimates of how many Westerners, these foreign fighters, are in ISIS ranks, and potentially thousands that we do not know who they are.

One of the biggest worries from a counterterrorism perspective is the unknown terrorists, those with no criminal record or intelligence traces, who could use a valid U.S. passport or the Visa Waiver Program to enter and exit the homeland.

For example, in May, a 22-year-old Florida man who joined al-Nusra in Syria, an al-Qaeda affiliate, killed 16 people and himself in a suicide bombing attack against Syrian government forces. U.S. officials say he was on their radar screen, but acknowledged that he traveled back to the United States before returning to Syria without detection.

It is also key for the administration to take the real steps to stop the radicalization of our youth so that they do not leave for jihad. This week, I visited the CBP's National Targeting Center to observe the hard-working men and women who are responsible for preventing travel by terrorists and those with terrorists ties and others who we have on various watch lists. The work they do targeting obscure information and connecting the dots to keep dangerous people out of the United States is vital to stopping ISIS.

Let me say I am hopeful—I am very hopeful that tonight—and I have talked to the Secretary, Jeh Johnson—I am very hopeful that tonight, we will hear from the President to take the advice of his chairman of Joint Chiefs, General Dempsey, that the only way you can defeat ISIS is to attack them wherever they exist. I am hopeful tonight that the President will come out strongly on the issue because it is a matter of National security, and it is a matter of homeland security that we do so, that we stop them over there before they can come here.

That is really the whole purpose of this hearing, one flight away, because these individuals are just one flight away. So I would like to ask the panel—you know, we have seen this gentleman from Florida get in and out undetected. We saw Tamerlan Tsarnaev, who was on the radar, get—leave this country and come back and pull off a terrorist attack in Boston.

What assurances can you give me that that will not happen in the future, Mr. Wagner?

Mr. WAGNER. Thank you. So looking at the lessons we learned with Tsarnaev and looking at—you know, we had access to certain pieces of information, and certain pieces of information, you know, weren't—weren't reading or actions being followed up in closing a lot of those gaps. We learned a real hard lesson with the Christmas day bomber. Here was a guy that we had in our sights, but you know, not really realizing his intentions at the time. We were waiting for him on the ground.

You know, taking a look at those procedures and getting—connecting better the pieces of information we have and taking action against a person as far in advance of them boarding that plane as possible, whether that is revoking their visa so when they check in with the airline, the airline is not able to print a boarding pass because the ESTA has been revoked or the visa has been revoked, or having our pre-clearance officers overseas question and talk and search a person before they get on-board that aircraft, or IAP officers that are working in conjunction with the airlines and the foreign authorities to question people and talk to them and try to determine a person's intent.

You know, with all the systems that we have and all the data we collect, we can look for patterns, we can look for pieces of information. We can connect known pieces of information. But determining a person's intent is a really difficult, difficult challenge, one best brought—really uncovered by questioning a person and using our skills to be able to do that and our search authorities to be able to do that.

Chairman MCCAUL. Now, when I talked to the Secretary, we talked about these Visa Waiver Program countries, the ability to get more information and more data from these countries so that we do know more about these travelers—would you agree with that? Could that be—legislatively, would that help you?

Mr. WAGNER. Yes. As an operational organization, we are always looking for additional sources of information to help us paint a better picture of a traveler or if we can figure out what their intentions are by having access to additional information and how we would use it and what circumstances we would use it and how we would protect it. But yes, in general, I would agree with that.

Chairman McCAUL. I would like to ask Mr. Miller and Ms. Lasley on the intelligence side of the house—my biggest concern is we don't have sufficient intelligence, human intelligence, particularly in Syria, to identify the 100 to 200 Americans that are over there, that we don't have sufficient intelligence on these tens of thousands of foreign fighters that could board an airplane and come into the United States.

I know we are not in a Classified setting, but does that disturb you? Is it possible that some of these foreign fighters have actually returned to the United States, like the man from Florida, and are currently here? Mr. Miller.

Mr. MILLER. Chairman, yes, sir, it does concern us. We continue to look at the known terrorists, to look at travel patterns, to look at who they are connected to, to look at some of the data elements that we may be able to utilize to identify future people. We identify—we continue to work with the law enforcement and intelligence community to see if there is additional data elements that we can utilize to help us identify those folks. We continue to work with our foreign partners, as well.

But as you stated, we can give more of what we are doing in a Classified environment to put the full picture together.

Chairman McCAUL. Ms. Lasley.

Ms. LASLEY. Sir, I would agree with my colleague's comments. We don't have a fulsome picture in all cases. I think that is why our interaction with our foreign counterparts in particular is quite important, so that where they have citizens who are fighting there, we share those identities and that information with each other. I know the Department and our work with State Department, both DHS and State are working very closely to make all of that information known and shared.

Chairman McCAUL. That all sounds great, but when I ask the question, do we have a high degree of confidence as to who these people are over there, I am always not satisfied with the answer. I think the honest answer is we don't. I would urge this administration—and I am hopeful that the President tonight will articulate a policy, strong policy, since we have pulled out of Iraq completely without a Status of Forces Agreement, and left the vacuum here now that has developed into what is one of the biggest threats to the homeland and Iraq and Syria, that we regain that reconnaissance, that intelligence, and also that intelligence on the ground to determine who is over there so that we can stop them from coming back to the United States and killing Americans.

With that, Madam Chairwoman, I yield back.

Mrs. MILLER. I thank the Chairman for his very insightful questions and comments.

The Chairwoman now recognizes the gentleman from Pennsylvania, Mr. Barletta.

Mr. BARLETTA. Thank you, Madam Chairwoman.

We spent a lot of time today discussing the threat of Islamic State terrorists gaining entry into the United States, but I am also very concerned, as the rest of the committee, about those who may already be here. Last year, the Government's own nonpartisan fact checker, the Government Accountability Office, reported that the

Department of Homeland Security has lost track of roughly 1 million foreign visitors.

Mr. Miller, what steps is DHS taking to identify these individuals and ensure the American people that they are not affiliated with the Islamic State? Wouldn't the completion of a biometric entry/exit system help against this threat?

Mr. MILLER. We have over the last several years taken several steps, along with HSI or Immigration and Custom Enforcement to identify those that have overstayed and prioritize them through our automated targeting system. With respect to the biometric exit, I would yield to Mr. Wagner.

Mr. WAGNER. Thank you. You know, we are using the biographical data now we receive. We receive 100 percent of—from the airlines of everyone coming in and everyone flying out via commercial air——

Mr. BARLETTA. But we are not doing land entries and exits.

Mr. WAGNER. We are doing some of it at the land—like, you know, we are doing——

Mr. BARLETTA. Well, my problem with that is, is that if we are not doing it everywhere, we really don't know if somebody has left the country.

Mr. WAGNER. Absolutely. Those are the gaps we are trying to close. As far as the biometric piece, we set up a demo lab with our science and technology branch. It opened a few months ago. We invite everyone to come visit it up in Landover, Maryland. We have got some scientists there and some very, very intelligent people there helping test out what are the right biometrics to collect, to record that entry and then ultimately, that exit from the United States in the different challenging environments that we need to do it, and in real time.

So over the course of this year and into next year, we will be piloting different types of biometrics in this demonstration lab. We are looking to do a few tests at airports over the course of the next year, and then have a good pilot in place at the beginning of 2016 at a single airport with what we think will be the right technology that we would then expand to additional locations.

Mr. BARLETTA. We know that terrorist networks have been using our porous Southern Border and a broken immigration system to enter the United States. Hezbollah has been actively setting up terrorist networks in Latin America for decades now and are working with the Mexican drug cartels to move contraband into the United States. Al-Shabaab has reportedly been sending individuals through Central America, take advantage of our broken immigration system and claiming asylum upon entry, but never showing up for their hearings.

Ms. Lasley or Mr. Miller, what measures are the Department of Homeland Security taking to ensure that the Islamic State does not take similar advantage of our porous borders and broken immigration system? Is this border crisis that we are seeing with the unaccompanied minors a concern that now HHS are taking the minors and just dispersing them across the United States without the Governors or States or communities even knowing who these individuals are—if you can touch on that.

Ms. LASLEY. Sir, certainly, we have had a long-standing concern in the Department about known or suspected terrorists and groups moving in and out of all of our border areas. So we are continually looking at the information and the intelligence that we receive, determine credibility of that information. To date, we have not had credible reporting that either Hezbollah or any other terrorist group has been taking advantage of our borders to move individuals in and out.

It is something we are always looking for, but to date, we have not seen credible evidence of that.

Mr. BARLETTA. Well, just this week, I have introduced a bill that would stop the Federal Government from sending unaccompanied minors around the company into our schools, into our neighborhoods without any knowledge at all of what is happening. You know, I think we really need to look at what they are looking at as how to get into the United States and kill Americans.

So thank you.

Ms. JACKSON LEE. Madam Chairwoman, just an inquiry. Could you give the gentleman an additional 30 seconds so that I can pose a question to the gentleman?

Mrs. MILLER. Yes.

Ms. JACKSON LEE. I thank the gentleman. We have worked together on a number of issues. Do you have documentation that unaccompanied children ages 2 years old and 4 years old and 6 years old and 10 years old are, in fact, known terrorists that are spread throughout the Nation? Do you have present and knowing knowledge and documentation? Maybe we will have to look at your documentation in a SCIF, but do you have known documentation?

Mr. BARLETTA. No, I am not saying that we have known documentation that the unaccompanied minors were—85 percent of them are the ages of 14 to 17 are——

Ms. JACKSON LEE. But even——

Mr. BARLETTA [continuing]. Are known terrorists. But shouldn't we—shouldn't we consider that a threat, that we don't know anything about these individuals, and they are being sent around the United States, especially with the threat that is going on in Iraq with ISIS, with our known intelligence that they want to come to the United States? Don't you think that we are vulnerable without knowing that?

Ms. JACKSON LEE. Well, let me—let me thank the gentleman for——

Mrs. MILLER. All right, the time——

The Chairwoman will now recognize Mr. O'Rourke from Texas for his comments.

Mr. O'ROURKE. Thank you, Madam Chairwoman. Appreciate you bringing us together for this hearing today and assembling the panel that we have.

I want to clarify the response Ms. Lasley made to Mr. Barletta's question or comment and seek further clarity from any Member of the panel who would wish to offer it.

When a Member of the Congress says, we all know that terrorist networks are using our Southern Border to enter the United States, I think it is very important for all of us in our sworn responsibility to know whether or not that is a true statement.

I have been told by DHS categorically as recently as last month that there is no evidence, nor has there ever been, of terrorists entering the United States from—through the Southern Border, our border with Mexico, or that terrorist plots have been foiled or intercepted at the Southern Border or that terrorist plots have been carried out within the United States that have a connection to the Southern Border. That is what I heard directly from DHS. Is there any further——

Mr. DUNCAN. Will the gentleman yield? Will the gentleman yield?

Mr. O'ROURKE. I will.

Mr. DUNCAN. An Iranian Quds Force operative tried to cross the Southern Border, contacted a—what he believed was a Mexican drug cartel. Turned out to be a DEA undercover operative in Mexico. His intent was to cross the Southern Border and bring nefarious objects with him to assassinate the ambassador from Saudi Arabia here in this city at a restaurant that you and I may have been attending that night.

Mr. O'ROURKE. Okay. I will——

Mr. DUNCAN. That is the facts. I just want to give you an example.

Mr. O'ROURKE. I will ask the experts at the panel to answer the question.

Ms. LASLEY. Sir, I would reiterate what I stated earlier, that we to-date don't have credible information, that we are aware of, of known or suspected terrorists coming across the border, particularly related to this threat stream or——

Mr. O'ROURKE. Any threat stream.

Ms. LASLEY [continuing]. Syrian foreign fighters.

Mr. O'ROURKE. Mr. Miller and Mr. Wagner, would you like to clarify what we have heard so far, either from Members of Congress or from your co-panelists?

Mr. WAGNER. Yes, thank you. Building upon that, the numbers of known watch-listed individuals that we have encountered at the ports, in between the ports on the Southwest Border is minimal compared to what we see in commercial aviation. You are talking tens versus thousands. It is minimal, from what we have seen from watch-listed encounters.

Mr. O'ROURKE. Okay. Mr. Miller.

Mr. MILLER. No, I would reiterate what Mr. Wagner said. In addition, we do have very robust information sharing with our counterparts in Central America, in Mexico, with the State and local partners. In fact, we are embedded in the Texas fusion center, our office of intelligence in Arizona. We have a robust intel structure, so we continue to look at this. When and if that sort of intel surfaced, we would take appropriate action.

Mr. O'ROURKE. Yes. I may submit a question for the record. I would like to share it with my colleagues the answers that I receive from you all. I would like to know, you know, once and for all what the facts support in terms of these repeated accusations that the Southern Border is unsafe, that terrorists are exploiting it to enter the United States. I want to make sure that we address the anecdote raised by my colleague from South Carolina. I think that is important, and I want to make sure that I know the truth on that.

This is not new, by the way. I am going to ask for consent to submit for the record *The El Paso Herald-Post* of Friday, December 17, 1981, "Border checked for Libyan hit squad." We have been projecting our anxiety——

Mrs. MILLER. Without objection.

[The information follows:]

ARTICLE SUBMITTED FOR THE RECORD BY HON. BETO O'ROURKE

BORDER CHECKED FOR LIBYAN "HIT SQUAD"

Inspectors report traffic moving as usual

by Patricia Lochraum and Jesse Tinsley

El Paso Herald-Post, Friday, December 17, 1981

Border inspectors reported business as usual today despite a careful lookout for members of a Libyan "hit squad" thought to be in Mexico.

Four Middle Eastern travelers have been stopped for further investigation since the alert began Monday, said Chief U.S. Customs Inspector Andy Towndrow today. None of the four were detained.

One border inspector has worn a bullet-proof vest for his bridge duties, but most of the customs inspectors in El Paso and along the Texas border simply stepped up routine inspections of passports, cars and purchases, officials said.

"It's not exciting to us," said customs inspector Rocky Galarra, 20, at the Bridge of the Americas port-of-entry.

"To us it is just dangerous. We don't get any kind of glory feeling about this, we just use extra caution."

The search has been complicated by Christmas shoppers, who have swelled the daily average number of cars or on foot, said regional U.S. Customs spokesman Charles Conroy in Houston. The amount increases significantly during the Christmas season, he added.

Some 1,270 Customs inspectors cover that traffic in Texas and New Mexico. The INS staff for Texas includes 78 people for the three El Paso ports.

"We can't afford to take this lightly," said Customs director Manny Najera, whose runs from Fort Hancock to Columbus N.M. "So we decided to tighten up and check passports and anything else that caught our attention."

El Paso offices now have composite sketched of the subjects and background information. But the distribution was so slow in some areas that border officials depended on newspapers for their sketches.

"We've seen more on television than we've gotten from the government," said Mitchell Britt, INS officer in charge at Laredo bridges.

Fred Aoyen, assistant regional commissioner for U.S. Customs in Houston, said the information flow had been as rapid as possible "without disrupting the national security."

Alan Giufni, INS district director in El Paso, said the major local impact of the extra checks had been a stackup of Christmas traffic.

If border officials found someone suspicious attempting to enter the country, they would alert local FBI agents, Najera said. The FBI declined to comment on the situation.

U.S. Consul Keith Powell at the U.S. Consulate General in Juarez declined comment when asked if he had received any information about the "hit team."

Some Federal officials were quoted Thursday saying that Arab communities along the border might be sounded for rumors about the squad. However, a Lebanese restaurant owner in a sizeable Middle Eastern community in Juarez said local feeling is that if the squad exists and is trying to cross into the U.S., El Paso would not be the city they choose.

"It's harder to cross from Juarez than it would be from Tijuana, our people feel," said George Yanor, 42. "We hear a lot of talk, but absolutely nothing about anyone coming into this area."

Mr. O'ROURKE [continuing]. Thank you, Madam Chairwoman— about threats to the United States on the U.S./Mexico border for as long as I have been alive. It does not mean that we should not be vigilant. It does not mean we should not take these threats seriously. But it does mean that we should only traffic in the facts and the data, and we should only raise these kinds of fears and anxieties when there is—there are facts to support them. So I just would ask for my colleagues to do that.

There are a number of questions I have. Most of them would probably be more appropriate in a Classified hearing. Here is a general one, and with time permitting, would love to get everyone's answer.

We are at war in Iraq right now. We have service members flying missions over there. We have boots on the ground and advisers. We are about to formalize that war, perhaps to some greater degree, after the President's speech tonight and potentially with Congressional action.

What does a greater state of war in Iraq and Syria mean to you in the jobs that you do? What additional resources, as the Ranking Member asked earlier, authorities and procedures would you need to meet additional threats following a greater U.S. involvement in those two countries?

I don't know if we can just have one of you answer just briefly. I am out of time. So with the Chairwoman's permission, would love another 30 seconds to hear from Ms. Lasley.

Ms. LASLEY. Sir, I would say that we have an imperative, and that imperative increases as the threat increases, to share information so that we can identify and stop individuals who want to come to this country, whether that is with our foreign partners, whether that is within the intelligence community or whether that is with our State and local law enforcement. So I think we will just continue to be very vigilant in making sure that that information is broadly shared.

Mr. O'ROURKE. Thank you. Yield back.

Mrs. MILLER. Thank you very much.

The Chairwoman now recognizes the gentleman from Florida, Mr. Clawson.

Mr. CLAWSON. Thank you for the work you do. Thanks for coming and being willing to sit in the crossfire a little bit and for your efforts to keep us safe.

As I went through my own preparation for today's meeting, it felt like the VWP is yesterday's tool for today's world. So at a 20,000-foot level, the question that kept coming to my mind as I worked it with my team—do we optimize yesterday's tool for today's world, or do we need to go to a new program altogether?

Maybe that means, you know, at one end of the continuum would be visas for everyone, could be less restrictive for that, would be more costly than what we currently do, and would probably—we would hear some pushback from the tourism industry and others.

I am not taking a position on that, but what I would like is for you to take a position on whether you feel we should optimize yesterday's tool for today's world, or do we need to break the mold a bit here and look for something more current?

Implied in my question, of course, is bang for buck. How much are we spending? How do we measure what we get for those expenses? I understand 300 caught, but I know you have more sophisticated ways of measuring what we are getting for our resources in this effort.

So I would like to hear all four of you answer how you feel whether we ought to continue this current road, whether we can see around corners good enough with this information, or do we need to go to a new level to protect the future?

Start with Mr. Miller. Thank you.

Mr. MILLER. Sir, I would agree with you. I think given a threat, we need to look at the information we are currently collecting, whether it is in the Visa Waiver Program or other avenues, and then—and take the appropriate action and decide if we need more information to collect.

As Mr. Wagner pointed out earlier, as operators using our targeting system, generally, more information is better as long as we can collect it in the right way, given civil rights, civil liberties, privacy, and we are able to operationalize it.

Mr. WAGNER. I would just say that, you know, VWP is an important program. It does get us information-sharing agreements and allows our close allies to share very important information with us that we are not getting from countries we don't have a VWP agreement with. You know, it requires them to issue electronic passports, which helps secure the documents, requires them to report lost and stolen passports to us.

So there are other benefits of what the overall program does get us access to and some visibility into. Like Mr. Miller mentioned, you know, we are taking a hard look at, are we collecting, you know, the right data elements and what other information could we make use of, and how would we collect it, you know, as we are with many of our programs.

But I think the program does have value, and you know, but a good review and a side-by-side of what VWP versus the visa program, you know, would offer and what types of benefits is always a good study to undertake.

Mr. CLAWSON. Are we doing it? Is anybody doing that?

Mr. WAGNER. Sir, we are reviewing the ESTA program. We are reviewing a lot of our different programs, you know, as we constantly do in light of the different threats that arise. You know, are there gaps in there? Are there gaps in the data collection? Are there gaps in how we connect our systems? So yes, we are looking at a lot of these things.

Ms. LASLEY. Sir, and I would say that that is across the Department. So the Department leadership is really looking at all the tools that we have in our toolkit and how we can optimize them to make sure that we have got the data that we need and that we are stopping people from coming into the country who shouldn't be here.

One of the tools that we have—if I could just highlight one that I think we are really trying to optimize is our watch-listing effort. So we are making a concerted effort within the Department to share as much of our Departmental data with our colleagues in the intelligence community to make sure that individuals are, in fact, put on the watch list.

We at I&A are responsible for that program on behalf of the DNI, and we do that for the entire Department, working with our colleagues at CBP, TSA, and others. Over the last 3 years, we have significantly increased the number of nominations that we in the Department have given to the intelligence community from about 4,000 2 years ago to well over 9,000 this year.

So that is one example of how we are trying to optimize a tool that we have in order to stop travelers from coming.

Ms. JOHNSON. As I mentioned, we have our information-sharing agreement with Visa Waiver Program partners. We are increasing and strengthening those information-sharing agreements and arrangements. In addition to beyond Visa Waiver Program, we are expanding the number of those agreements, and we work very closely with our interagency partners on that watch-listing information to make sure our foreign partners have that information, as well. I think those are very strong tools.

Mr. CLAWSON. I urge you and I urge us to look at secondary and incremental and more than incremental efforts in this—in what we are doing here. I am a user of global entry for my business before I came here. It makes me nervous that you all interview me, but you don't interview people that could be face-to-face that could be somewhere in Europe that could be wanting to come to our country. To my knowledge, I don't think we do that. Am I right about that, in the current ESTA program?

Mr. WAGNER. They would get interviewed upon arrival in the United States by a CBP Officer, but there is no interview to issue that ESTA unless we have a—they come through a pre-clearance location, where we would interview them before they got on-board the plane, or unless some of our targeting systems and some of our analysis of their reservation data gave us cause for, you know, some type of reason to have our immigration advisory program officers, if they are coming through one of those 11 locations, talk to them before boarding and address any types of questions we have.

So the possibility is there. We are in a lot of VWP countries. We are in, you know, London Heathrow. We are in Manchester. We are in Paris. We are in Amsterdam. We are in Frankfurt, you know, major gateways, major, you know, places of travel, especially for VWP travelers. So we have the opportunity if our other systems do flag them for additional review or scrutiny.

Mr. CLAWSON. Well, if you do a face-to-face with me, I would really love you to do it with potential bad guys coming from outside our country, as well.

Thank you for your answers. Yield back.

Mrs. MILLER. Thank the gentleman.

The Chairwoman now recognizes the gentleman from South Carolina, Mr. Duncan.

Mr. DUNCAN. Thank you, Madam Chairwoman.

Thank the panel for being here today and for your service to our country.

In February 2014, this year, the director of national intelligence, James Clapper, started out testifying before the Senate Armed Services Committee by saying, "looking back over my now more than half a century in intelligence, I have not experienced a time when we have been beset by more crises and threats around the globe."

Two days ago, we have a staff meeting on fly-in day, and I shared a video with my staff of—there was an ISIS-produced video, but it showed young Iraqi men loaded in the back of pick-up trucks and dump trucks taken out into the desert and murdered, hundreds of Iraqis. It hearkened to times of Pol Pot in Cambodia and the Holocaust to watch those images that were disturbing of men shot multiple times to make sure they were dead as they laid in the trench!

This is a real threat. We may not think as Americans that we may not be interested in Islamic extremism and ISIS and the establishment of a caliphate, but I will tell you what. ISIS is interested in America, and they are interested in you.

In June, I traveled to Europe on a codel, and I couldn't get many Members of Congress interested in going. We were looking at border security and foreign fighter flow—in June. If I was to have that same Congressional delegation trip today, I would have to turn Members away because the plane wouldn't be big enough to travel to Europe to meet with our allies about foreign fighter flow.

I grew up during the cold war, nation-state versus nation-state, tracking the movements of tanks and large numbers of troops along different borders in mainly Eastern Europe. We are not tracking troop movement or tank movement today, we are tracking individuals, foreign fighters who leave not only European countries but this country to travel to fight jihad, ofttimes being radicalized and coming back possibly to the United States of America to create and commit heinous crimes.

Is that a far-fetched idea? Well, before I left to travel to Brussels, a young man who had traveled to Syria through Turkey came back through Germany. Germany tracked his movements but failed to let the allies within Europe know about this individual. He entered Brussels. He shot up a Jewish museum. At least three if not four individuals were killed. Have you heard about that on the mainstream media in this country? Probably not. I knew about it because I was headed to Brussels and it was on our radar screen.

But this was a jihadist fighter who radicalized, came back to Brussels, shot up a Jewish museum, killed individuals and tried to flee back to North Africa through France. He was caught at a bus stop.

Free travel, shingen region in Europe, free travel among those countries, no border crossings. Guess what? They are visa waiver countries, as well. If they didn't know that individual had actually traveled to Syria and become radicalized, if he would have been— a country that was part of the Visa Waiver Program, traveled back to his country unbeknownst to the United States personnel, had a valid travel document, possibly could have boarded an aircraft and flown to this country.

We need to be concerned about that. We also need to be concerned about Americans. We now have identified a number that have traveled over to fight with ISIS, whether it is in Syria or Iraq or the Islamic State and whatever it looks like going forward. We should be able to revoke the passports of United States citizens if they do travel to fight for another organization.

In fact, U.S. law under—I guess it is Section 8 U.S.C. 1481 says that a U.S. citizen shall lose its nationality by volunteering and performing any of the following acts: Entering or serving in the armed forces of a foreign state. Now, there is a part of the law that says with the intention of relinquishing United States nationality. Maybe we need to strike that in future law.

But if you go on "and committing any act of treason against or attempting to force the overthrow or bearing arms against the United States"—that is exactly what ISIS and ISIL have said. If you go on to other laws, we can revoke a United States passport if the Secretary receives certification from a State agency that an individual owes arrears of child support in excess of $2,500.

We can revoke their passport just because they don't pay child support, but you can't tell me we are going to revoke the passports of people that are going to fight with people in ISIS that have said, we are coming to the White House, we are going to fly that black ISIS-al-Qaeda flag over the White House, who have made threats to the United States, who have beheaded two American journalists? But we can revoke their passport if they fail to pay their child support?

Secretary shall issue the passport—let's just go on to say, the Supreme Court has interpreted Passport Act of 1926 that gives broad powers to the Secretary to revoke a passport when necessary for security purposes.

We need to revoke the passports of these Americans that have gone. We need to keep them from reentering the United States when we know who they are. We need to understand, America, the challenges of tracking individuals, foreign fighters, and as they flow around the world through even some allied countries, where they end up.

Madam Chairwoman, this is an apropos committee hearing. I hope this isn't the last one. We have got a lot of threats facing our country. I hope that the President comes out strongly tomorrow night against this threat to the United States of America and the very freedoms that we enjoy.

With that, I yield back.

Mrs. MILLER. Thank the gentleman, very much.

I think we are all very interested to hear what the President has to say about this issue. I think it is—I would guess, certainly in my district, and I think most Members when they were home in their districts over the last month, we heard about this ISIS threat over and over and over being talked about. It certainly has—I think the Nation understands and is looking for the President to— he is the commander-in-chief—to outline to the country how serious of a threat it is, and what we need to be doing as a country to address it.

Really, the purpose of this hearing——

Ms. JACKSON LEE. Madam Chairwoman?

Mrs. MILLER. In a moment. Really, the purpose of this hearing was to talk about what we can do legislatively to assist all of you. As I mentioned, I have currently two different bills that we are looking at and introducing. I would also encourage all of you—for instance, Mr. Wagner, you mentioned that you are looking, you are reviewing, as you always are, about changes in ESTA, what kinds of things would be helpful.

Please keep us in the information loop. You don't have to wait until we have a hearing to let us know what you are doing. I know that maybe what you are looking at doing is better talked about in the SCIF, but in a Classified situation, but still, please keep us in the information loop.

Does the Ranking Member have a comment?

Ms. JACKSON LEE. I do, thank you very much, very briefly. Let me just hope to make sure that Ms. Lasley responds to my question and to just put on the record that there is a, I think, looming question of watch list, No-Fly List. I think this hearing should leave the American public with the idea that we are being vigilant and that we are knowledgeable that ISIL wants to form an Islamic state, but we balance that with our civil liberties and facts.

So I would ask for the—anyone who may have documentation—I guess it is in different jurisdictions, but I want to just put on the record—documentation on the status or the type of unaccompanied children. I would like to get that report from anybody who has access to that.

I would like to yield 15 seconds to—and thank the witnesses very much, too—Mr. O'Rourke, very briefly.

Mr. O'ROURKE. Thank you——

Mrs. MILLER. You don't have to yield to him. I will recognize the gentleman.

Mr. O'ROURKE. Thank you, Madam Chairwoman.

My colleague and friend from South Carolina, when I asked about a connection to known terrorist plots and the U.S./Mexico border, mentioned the Iran terror plot to assassinate somebody here in Washington, DC. There is, in fact, from everything that I know about this, absolutely no connection to the border. In fact, the plotter was interdicted at JFK airport, where he was arrested due to our coordination with the government of Mexico. The person with whom he thought he was dealing was actually a DEA agent posing as a cartel member.

The border was never exploited. While I think this is a serious issue, and again, one against which we must remain vigilant, there is no connection to the border. So I invite anyone, and especially those who have the subject-matter expertise, to tell me if I am wrong. But my understanding is that the border is as secure as it has ever been, and we do not have any known terror plots tied to the border. Doesn't mean that there might not be some, doesn't mean we shouldn't guard against it, but let's again deal in the facts.

Mrs. MILLER. All right, I thank the gentleman for his comments. I think I would yield to the gentleman—or recognize the gentleman from South Carolina, if you would like to respond.

Mr. DUNCAN. I thank the gentleman. I think that the Iranian threat was to come across the Southern Border. It was thwarted before it ever happened. So you are right and wrong.

I will say this. We have no idea who is in our country. For us not to recognize that we have open borders and that we have no idea who has entered our country illegally and what their intentions were—whether it was an intention to get a job and provide for their family or whether it was an intention to maybe create a terrorist cell and do something nefarious in the future, we don't know.

I met with the security force of the King Ranch in your State, 30, 40 miles north of Brownsville, 837,000 acres. It is as large as the State of Rhode Island. So they have got their own security force. This was 2 years ago. He said, Mr. Duncan, we are catching on our property some OTMs. OTM now is a term that is only being applied, in the press anyway, to unaccompanied children from countries other than Mexico, such as El Salvador, Nicaragua, Honduras, Guatemala. But before that, OTM meant anyone that wasn't of Mexican descent.

He said, Mr. Duncan, we are catching folks on our property that are African, that are Asian, and that are Middle Eastern. This is 50 miles north of the border. They came across the border illegally.

I just met with a Secret Service agent on the sidewalk in Washington that was riding a bike, former military guy, served nine tours in Afghanistan. That ought to tell you what he did in the military. He said part of his training was on the Southern Border watching, and they saw thousands of people come across the border, they called CBP and nobody showed up.

He said, part of our work was radio and communications intercept, because they were getting ready to go do the same thing in Afghanistan. He said, everything we heard was not Spanish.

Wake up, America! With a porous Southern Border, we have no idea who is in our country.

I yield back.

Mrs. MILLER. Thank the gentleman. I thank everyone for their passion on this issue. Obviously, there is a lot of interest in this. I certainly want to thank all of the witnesses for their testimony today. I know some of the questions that were asked will be—their—you know, answers will be submitted in writing to the committee. We appreciate that. With that——

Ms. JACKSON LEE. Thank you, Madam Chairwoman. I just want to say thank you. I know that you are ending. I just want to say that this is a committee of facts. No one knows and has documented that those OTMs were terrorists. I yield back.

Mrs. MILLER. I appreciate that.

Ms. JACKSON LEE. Thank you.

Mrs. MILLER. We would also mention that pursuant to the committee rule 7(c), the hearing record will be held open for 10 days. So without objection, the committee stands adjourned.

[Whereupon, at 11:53 a.m., the subcommittee was adjourned.]

APPENDIX

QUESTION FROM HONORABLE BETO O'ROURKE FOR TROY MILLER

Question. According to Deputy Under Secretary for Analysis Jennifer Lasley, to date, there is no credible information that indicates that known or suspected terrorists have entered through the U.S. border, from either Hezbollah or other terrorist groups, including ISIL or Syrian foreign fighters. However, there are repeated accusations that the Southern U.S. Border is unsafe. What intelligence has the U.S. Department of Homeland Security (DHS) or the U.S. Department of State collected that may demonstrate whether or not a known or suspected terrorist individual(s) or group(s) has entered through the U.S. borders, specifically the U.S. Southern Border? Please provide this information in a Classified and/or Unclassified manner.

Answer. Response was not received at the time of publication.

QUESTION FROM HONORABLE BETO O'ROURKE FOR JOHN P. WAGNER

Question. According to Deputy Under Secretary for Analysis Jennifer Lasley, to date, there is no credible information that indicates that known or suspected terrorists have entered through the U.S. border, from either Hezbollah or other terrorist groups, including ISIL or Syrian foreign fighters. However, there are repeated accusations that the Southern U.S. Border is unsafe. What intelligence has the U.S. Department of Homeland Security (DHS) or the U.S. Department of State collected that may demonstrate whether or not a known or suspected terrorist individual(s) or group(s) has entered through the U.S. borders, specifically the U.S. Southern Border? Please provide this information in a Classified and/or Unclassified manner.

Answer. Response was not received at the time of publication.

QUESTION FROM HONORABLE BETO O'ROURKE FOR JENNIFER A. LASLEY

Question. According to Deputy Under Secretary for Analysis Jennifer Lasley, to date, there is no credible information that indicates that known or suspected terrorists have entered through the U.S. border, from either Hezbollah or other terrorist groups, including ISIL or Syrian foreign fighters. However, there are repeated accusations that the Southern U.S. Border is unsafe. What intelligence has the U.S. Department of Homeland Security (DHS) or the U.S. Department of State collected that may demonstrate whether or not a known or suspected terrorist individual(s) or group(s) has entered through the U.S. borders, specifically the U.S. Southern Border? Please provide this information in a Classified and/or Unclassified manner.

Answer. Response was not received at the time of publication.

QUESTION FROM HONORABLE BETO O'ROURKE FOR HILLARY BATJER JOHNSON

Question. According to Deputy Under Secretary for Analysis Jennifer Lasley, to date, there is no credible information that indicates that known or suspected terrorists have entered through the U.S. border, from either Hezbollah or other terrorist groups, including ISIL or Syrian foreign fighters. However, there are repeated accusations that the Southern U.S. Border is unsafe. What intelligence has the U.S. Department of Homeland Security (DHS) or the U.S. Department of State collected that may demonstrate whether or not a known or suspected terrorist individual(s) or group(s) has entered through the U.S. borders, specifically the U.S. Southern Border? Please provide this information in a Classified and/or Unclassified manner.

Answer. We are alert to the possibility that terrorist groups and their supporters, including groups such as the Islamic State in Iraq and the Levant (ISIL), Hezbollah, and HAMAS, might view the Southern U.S. Border as a feasible means to enter the United States.

ISIL currently poses a threat to the people of Iraq and Syria, and the broader Middle East—including American citizens, personnel, and facilities overseas. If left unchecked, it could pose a growing threat beyond that region, including to the United States. While we have not yet detected specific plotting against our homeland, ISIL leaders have threatened America and our allies. Our intelligence community believes that thousands of foreigners, including Europeans and some Americans, have joined them in Syria and Iraq. Trained and battle-hardened, these fighters could try to return to their home countries and carry out deadly attacks.

However, there is no credible information suggesting current ISIL, Hezbollah, HAMAS, or other violent Islamist extremist individuals or groups have entered through the U.S. Southern Border. Furthermore, there is no credible evidence of current ties between Mexican organized crime groups and domestic or these international terrorist groups, and there is no indication that these terrorist organizations use Mexico as an entry point to the United States. We continue to monitor the region for signs of an increased threat.

The United States has strengthened our overall law enforcement cooperation with Mexican authorities. This cooperation, combined with the Mexican government's efforts to address its own internal law enforcement challenges and to more effectively police its borders, north and south, should help to make the region, including our shared border, safer and more secure.

○